D

Books are to be returned on or before
the last date below.

LIBREX-

The British Computer Society

BCS is the leading professional body for the IT industry. With members in over 100 countries, BCS is the professional and learned Society in the field of computers and information systems.

The BCS is responsible for setting standards for the IT profession. It is also leading the change in public perception and appreciation of the economic and social importance of professionally managed IT projects and programmes. In this capacity, the Society advises, informs and persuades industry and government on successful IT implementation.

IT is affecting every part of our lives and that is why BCS is determined to promote IT as the profession of the 21st century.

Joining BCS

BCS qualifications, products and services are designed with your career plans in mind. We not only provide essential recognition through professional qualifications but also offer many other useful benefits to our members at every level.

BCS membership demonstrates your commitment to professional development. It helps to set you apart from other IT practitioners and provides industry recognition of your skills and experience. Employers and customers increasingly require proof of professional qualifications and competence. Professional membership confirms your competence and integrity and sets an independent standard that people can trust. Professional Membership (MBCS) is the pathway to Chartered IT Professional (CITP) status.

www.bcs.org/membership

Further Information

Further information about BCS can be obtained from: The British Computer Society, First Floor, Block D, North Star House, North Star Avenue, Swindon, SN2 1FA, UK.

Telephone: 0845 300 4417 (UK only) or + 44 (0)1793 417 424 (overseas)

Contact: www.bcs.org/contact

Exploiting IT for Business Benefit

Bob Hughes

The right of Bob Hughes to be identified as author of this Work has been asserted by him/her in accordance with sections 77 and 78 of the Copyright, Designs and Patents Act 1988.

The British Computer Society
Publishing and Information Products
First Floor, Block D
North Star House
North Star Avenue
Swindon
SN2 1FA
UK

www.bcs.org

ISBN 978-1-902505-92-3

British Cataloguing in Publication Data.
A CIP catalogue record for this book is available at the British Library.

Typeset by Lapiz Digital.
Printed at CPI Anthony Rowe.

Contents

List of figures and tables

Author

Bob Hughes was born on the Isle of Sheppey in Kent. He worked in various IT development roles – from software developer to project leader – in the telecommunications, energy and local government sectors, until moving to the University of Brighton where he is a principal lecturer. Previous books include *Software Project Management*, published by McGraw-Hill and currently in its fifth edition, with Indian and Chinese versions. He contributed and edited the BCS publication *Project Management for IT-related Projects*. He is the Systems subject moderator for the BCS professional examinations and chair of the ISEB project management examination panel. His current major interest is in interactive and collaborative elearning, particularly to support greater understanding of the practical problems of implementing IT in business environments.

Abbreviations

ABC	activity-based costing
ABM	activity-based management
ASP	Active Server Pages
ASP	application service providers
B2B	business to business
B2C	business to consumer
BoB	best of breed
BPR	business process re-engineering
COTS	customized off-the-shelf
CRM	customer relationship management
DCF	discounted cash flow
DTD	Document Type Definition
EAI	enterprise application integration
EDI	Electronic Data Interchange
ERP	enterprise resource planning
e-SCM	web-enabled supply chain management
EU	European Union
GIS	geographical information system
GPS	global positioning system
GRN	goods received note
HTML	HyperText Markup Language
HTTP	HyperText Transfer Protocol
IP	Internet Protocol
IS	information systems
IT	information technology
JSP	Java Server Pages

MRP II	manufacturing resource planning
MRP	materials requirements planning
NPV	net present value
OGC	Office of Government Commerce
OTS	off-the-shelf
P2P	person to person
PEU	perceived ease of use
POS	point of sale
PU	perceived usefulness
RFC	Requests for Comments
RFID	radio frequency identification
ROI	return on investment
SEO	search engine optimization
SOAP	Simple Object Access Protocol
TCP	Transmission Control Protocol
TTF	task-technology fit
UDDI	Universal Description, Discovery and Integration
URI	Universal Resource Identifier
URL	Uniform Resource Locator
VDU	visual display unit
WSDL	Web Service Description Language
XML	eXtensible Markup Language
XSD	XML Schema Definition

Preface

The quotation above echoes many comments from the business community about the apparent lack of understanding by some IT professionals of the business context in which they work. This concern for common understanding is shared by the BCS which, for example, believes that computing students on BCS accredited courses should have a full appreciation of the economic implications of information systems. The early development of computers – particularly in the UK where the landmark LEO series of computers was developed, made and sold by Lyons, a company which originally built the machines to support its bakery and catering business – was characterized by an engagement between business and technical expertise. This introductory text aims to give computing and information systems (IS) professionals a greater insight into the business context in which IT is developed and deployed. It attempts to explore the concerns that motivate business people when they try to define what they want from information technologists.

Some blame the way universities teach computing as one of the causes of the apparent gap in the understanding between customer-facing business and IT. While I believe that such criticism is not completely fair – in my own institution the large majority of undergraduate students spend one year of their four-year course working on placement in industry – there is an element of truth in the charge. Some computer specialists, many of whom are highly regarded in their subject discipline, fail to see much of value in addressing topics beyond the production of software that meets a precise specification. One hope in producing this publication is to persuade some colleagues that the study of the interplay between computer systems and the wider world – which is hugely broader than the matter of interface design – can be intellectually stimulating, challenging and rewarding, even for those who might regard themselves as primarily computer scientists or software engineers.

Some in large business corporations have made the effort, through organizations such as eSkills UK, to identify what IT professionals should know about business, and by extension what, in their view, computing students should be taught. While this makes a valuable and challenging contribution to syllabus development, this is not enough to build a coherent and structured body of knowledge. Many specialist disciplines in business outside IT would understand that such bodies of knowledge have to be developed carefully over time, supported by verifiable evidence and made comprehensible and consistent through the creation of models and theories. This book, for example, draws upon models such as Michael Porter's model of competitive forces and Everett Rogers' models of the diffusion of innovation. It is hoped that this book can make a very modest but positive contribution to the debate on the nature of the discipline of business information systems.

The idea of 'ebusiness strategy' needs to be explained. The term ecommerce predates ebusiness and describes the buying and selling of goods and services online, which increasingly means via the internet. Ebusiness is a broader term than ecommerce and relates to the use of electronic means to carry out business. Usually the internet is involved but, as will be seen in Chapter 6, some internal computer processes might not use the internet but are essential to enable online transactions. Hence a broad view has been taken that all IT processes are within the scope of this book.

Until quite recently, teaching or training in IT strategy concepts to any but high-level executives concerned with the long-term direction of an organization has seemed pointless. Ebusiness, particularly the use of the internet to conduct business, has, however, transformed the place of IT in organizations. From being hidden in the depths of an organization, an organization now has IT systems that are on display to the outside world. This includes customers through business to consumer (B2C) applications and suppliers and business partners through business to business (B2B) applications. Once an IT system was a hidden back office process that simply recorded the actions of customer-facing staff; now it is increasingly the medium through which customers see and talk to an organization. Strategic business concerns were once remote from IT professionals; now these staff are becoming responsible for strategic activities.

If readers expect the material in this book to be about developing some sort of master plan that specifies, step by step, the route to an organizational objective, then they will be disappointed, although we do discuss topics such as the planning and management of programmes of business change. There is a view that is increasingly accepted that while it is essential to have long-term objectives that are clearly described and widely communicated, the steps by which the objectives are to be achieved may have to be improvised to meet the constantly changing demands and opportunities of the real world. I confess that in this book there is a tendency to use the term 'strategy' rather broadly to refer to the business motivations behind a particular deployment of IT.

A common theme in writings on IT strategy has been the need for true business need to drive the adoption of elements of IT. It is unarguable that IT should support business needs and that adopting technology for its own sake can be counter-productive. However, it is simplistic to suggest that management should formulate their initial business strategies in an abstract world with no consideration of technologies. The development of many technologies has had huge unforeseen consequences and often seems to have transformed the world we live in with a momentum that seems independent of any one organizing and controlling entity. One element of strategic planning will need to be the scrutiny of new technologies to see what opportunities and threats they pose for the business.

In researching and preparing this book, I have become increasingly aware of the debts I owe not just to those who have contributed directly to this work, but to colleagues who over the years have contributed to my general understanding of the subject. These include, among my current and former colleagues, Mike Cotterell, Dave King, Marian Eastwood, Pavle Bataveljic, David Coutinho, Heinz Seefried and Jon Dron. Particular thanks also go to colleagues in the Brighton Business School, including Laurence Olver, Kevin Turner, Clare Millington, Cliff Conway and Asher Rospigliosi, who by collaborating in the teaching of business concepts to computing students in such an open and helpful way have also helped to educate at least some computing staff. I have also learnt much, especially some good sources of information and new ideas, from colleagues at Nottingham Trent University and the University of the West of England where I have been an external examiner – although perhaps I should not admit this. Other sources of business education have been students who have often helped by identifying useful sources and by talking about their placement experiences. Masters students, such as Andrew Crossey and Louisa Segenhout, provided useful insights from their work environments through their project reports. There are also, of course, the businesses with whom we have worked in research, training and student work placement activities. In this respect, Trevor Marshal at the Royal & Sun Alliance and Alan Cunliffe at Ericsson were particularly good enablers and facilitators.

I would like to acknowledge the forbearance of Heather, Katherine and Tom not just in relation to the writing of this book but also generally.

1 The Internet, the Web and Business Opportunity

LEARNING OUTCOMES

When you have completed this chapter you should be able to demonstrate an understanding of the following:

- why IT specialists need an understanding of business strategy;
- the impact of the internet and web on the ways in which information systems are designed and developed;
- the characteristics of the internet and the web that have made them so pervasive;
- the ways in which revenues can be generated by web applications.

INTRODUCTION

> 'To survive you have to stop being seen as a technology person and start being seen as a business person.'
> Myron Hrycyk, head of IT Unipart Automotive Logistics (quoted in *Computing Business* November 2005, page 21).

Many observers have commented on the need within the business world for IT practitioners who not only have a grasp of modern information and communication technologies but also an understanding of the way that organizations use these technologies.

The relationship between IT and business has been transformed in the last decade or so by the almost universal adoption of internet and web technologies. This has moved an organization's IT from being a backroom operation, hidden from the outside world, to being its shop window. This makes the design and development of IT systems which fulfil business needs even more important.

The motivation of this book is to bridge the gap between IT and business understanding. Every gap has two sides. IT professionals certainly need to be aware of business needs. However, it is important that business specialists are aware of how new technologies can present often unexpected and unpredicted opportunities – as well as risks that can in extreme cases be fatal to a business. Many in the business world have, with some justification, complained about IT practitioners pursuing technological 'solutions' for their own sake rather than to support the goals of the business which employs them. Some have argued that business needs must be identified first and a strategy that fulfils those needs should then be devised. Only at this point, it is argued, should the role of IT in supporting these needs be considered. We argue that this approach is almost as blinkered as that of the computer geek. The availability of new technologies has been a constant driver for economic transformation since at least the time when the development of steam engines meant that woollen mills no longer had to be sited on rivers in order to have a source of power.

During the early decades of business computer development the focus was on automating existing clerical procedures. Business analysis and system design methods were usually based on the assumption that there were staff members who were carrying out the procedures that were to be computerized and they could be interrogated about their roles. A computer system was then designed that effectively mimicked these procedures. Today, there is often no existing system to be mimicked – new IT development is simultaneously business development. It can also be difficult to interrogate potential users of a system as many of these will be members of the public who have yet to identify themselves as possible visitors to your website.

In the remainder of this chapter we are going to explore briefly some of the key technical characteristics of the internet and the web that have contributed to their power to transform our world. We will look particularly at the characteristics that have encouraged ecommerce and ebusiness, and we will finish by looking at the revenue models that describe how money can be made from the web.

THE INTERNET AND THE WORLD WIDE WEB

A brief trip down memory lane

The internet provides an easy way to transfer data between computers. Not so long ago, computer screens were only ever seen in organizational environments where visual display units (VDUs) were attached to isolated mainframe computers. (In real life things were – and are – usually more complicated than a description of the basic technologies might suggest, so you need to understand that in places we will be simplifying matters to make them more straightforward to grasp.) This configuration meant that computer communication between users was, at best, limited to workers within the same organization. The general structure of the configuration was a star-shape – see Figure 1.1.

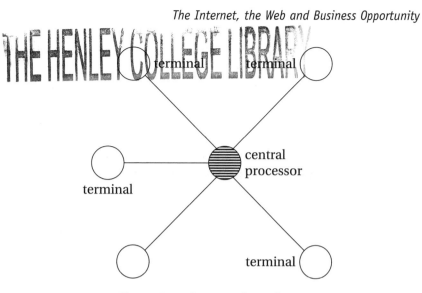

FIGURE 1.1   *A star configuration*

Generally speaking the communication lines between the computer and its terminals were commissioned and owned by the organization. Sometimes a user might be geographically remote and might be allowed to access the mainframe over the public telephone system – a **dial-up connection**. This was like making a normal phone call in that you paid for all the time that you had exclusive control of the channel, even though you might not be using it. It was possible to engineer a link between two mainframes but these usually needed dedicated lines.

> We are describing here the situation that existed in the late 1970s and early 1980s.

These arrangements had serious limitations. The first, as we saw above, was that communication was limited to people within the organization. Computer data could be transferred between organizations but this would often involve the physical delivery of magnetic tapes. Even this was not straightforward as different computer models (sometimes even those made by the same manufacturer) could have different data formats.

Another potential disadvantage was the vulnerability of the central computer at the heart of the star-node. If that went down then the network was dead. Associated with this were the restrictions the star configuration put on growth. The capacity of the central computer through which all communication travelled was a bottle-neck that constrained the number of terminals that could be added to the system.

The emergence of the internet

The vulnerability of the central processor was of particular concern for military planners in the United States at the time of the cold war, when the threat of a nuclear strike seemed very real. This motivated the design of a decentralized networked system to link computers where there was no single central processor, but a number of routers at various junctions in the network of communication lines – see Figure 1.2. If one pathway between two computers failed, an alternative pathway could be found. As well as being robust, this architecture was **scalable** – new nodes (that is, computers), lines and routers could be added with relative ease, leading to the universal system that we have today.

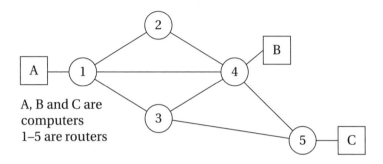

A, B and C are computers
1–5 are routers

FIGURE 1.2 *A network configuration*

ACTIVITY 1.1 THE NATURE OF NETWORKS

In Figure 1.2, how many possible routes are there between A and C which do not involve visiting the same router more than once en route? What is the minimum number of channels between routers that could be cut in order to isolate C? What would be the effect of this isolation on the remainder of the network?

The original method of communication between computers was by lines where the machines had sole use of these lines during the time when they might need to communicate. This can be a particularly wasteful use of a computer link, especially if a human user is involved who spends time fumbling over a QWERTY keyboard and not actually using the line efficiently. The solution to this was the use of **data packets**. Lines were not exclusively reserved for the use of two terminal nodes. Computer data was transmitted by the sending of a number of segments which were reassembled at the receiving end. Data packets belonging to different computer dialogues could be interspersed as they travelled around the network. This made the system much more efficient as a line could be simultaneously used by many different users, rather than being reserved for just one lucky pair.

We have already noted how different makes of computer could have very different architectures and operating systems and could even have different data formats. This means that the internet depends on agreement about how technologies are to interoperate. This is rather like a road transport system – such a system needs a physical structure but also agreement on how it is to be used, for example on which side of the road vehicles will be driven, what the procedures will be at crossroads and round-abouts and so on. In the computer world these conventions are known as **protocols**. A protocol is a particular form of standard, an agreed common way of doing something. Different computers could have different architectures but could communicate if both used the same protocols for this purpose, just as a Chinese airline pilot and a German air traffic controller can communicate by both speaking English when the plane is about to land.

ACTIVITY 1.2 ESTABLISHING STANDARDS

These days barcodes are used to identify goods in most shops that have point of sale (POS) equipment. What standards would have had to have been agreed for barcode systems to work in shops? Who would have needed to have been involved in the agreement of the standards?

Some standards have been enforced by governments and have a legal force. Governments, however, are local while commerce and communication are global. As a consequence some international bodies, such as the ISO, the International Standards Organization, have been established to obtain agreements on international standards. One problem for such organizations is that almost by definition the standards have to be based on agreement and consensus and this can be time-consuming to achieve, especially as there is national pride and competitive advantage involved with a particular national standard becoming international. Delays can also result from a natural desire that the standards should reflect best practice and the identification of this best practice can take time. While these negotiations are going on, the people on the ground have to find immediate solutions to their day-to-day problems and this is likely to lead to the emergence of imperfect, but workable, informal practices. One of the reasons for the rapid development and adoption of the internet was the relatively flexible and informal approach whereby standards were shaped through a series of Requests for Comments (RFCs) using a process with an emphasis on getting working implementations of proposals up and running quickly.

The internet is distinguished largely by two important protocols.

(i) **Transmission Control Protocol (TCP)** governs the way that computers sending and receiving data across the internet behave. It covers things like the way in which the data that is to be sent is broken down into packets and how they are then put together again at their destination.

(ii) **Internet Protocol (IP)** defines how routers pass the packets through the network.

5

Alternative ways of doing these things have been defined in competing protocols, some of which have come through the ISO, but in the end it has been the internet with its TCP/IP protocols that has become predominant.

The web

The web is separate from but dependent upon the internet. There are things that we can do with the internet that do not involve the web, the most obvious of which is sending email.

> FTP which is used for transferring files is another example of a non-web internet application.

The internet provides a means by which electronic data can be sent from one computer to another. However, the two computers would also need to have complementary software – the sender to create the data and the recipient to interpret and process it. For example, a computer might send a data record containing the string '0304193230092003M'. This string on the face of it means little or nothing, but the recipient computer may have software that interprets the data as two dates, 3 April 1932 and 30 September 2003 (which are the dates of birth and death of a certain male – hence the 'M'). This computer might then calculate the lifespan of the male in years, perhaps as part of some research into life expectancy. The two communicating systems need to share some kind of template which describes the format of the data.

> Electronic Data Interchange (EDI) is designed to facilitate B2B data transfer based on this model.

Things are in some ways a lot easier if the data is destined for a human rather than a machine: we can then use normal text – as in this book – and, hopefully, can convey meaning to the reader without the intervention of a machine.

Lots of useful information can be conveyed as text. Diagrams and pictures can be embedded in text. To reproduce a page of text, like this one, so that its overall appearance is maintained, some formatting information is required. This might include the fonts to be used, the places where the text will be indented and where new lines are to start (in the case of poetry and more prosaically lists), where there are gaps between lines and so on. Where the text is designed from the outset to be held electronically we can enhance it by adding **hypertext** features such as the ability to jump from one part of the document to another part or even to other documents. If there were some way by which this text could be retrieved from a distant computer along with formatting instructions that the requesting computer could use to reproduce the appearance of the original document, then this would constitute a powerful information tool. The two computers could have radically different architectures but if there was a standard way of representing text and formatting rules, then software applications that generated and presented data in the common format could be written for each hardware/software platform. Every computer regardless of design could then pass information to every other computer.

This, crudely, is what the web does. A key figure in the development of the web has been Tim Berners-Lee who invented the fundamentals of the web when he worked for CERN, the European Particle Physics Laboratory, based near Geneva in Switzerland. This laboratory conducts experiments probing the nature of matter which can involve literally hundreds of scientists from all over the globe, so it was an appropriate place for the birth of the web. The web is based on three protocols: **HyperText Transfer Protocol** (HTTP), **HyperText Markup Language** (HTML), and **Uniform Resource Locators** (URLs).

(i) HTTP defines the methods by which information is requested by one computer (the '**client**') from another (the '**server**') and by which the information is then sent back.

(ii) HTML is used for formatting text and other objects so that they can be represented in a predictable manner by a distant computer.

(iii) URLs provide an addressing mechanism that allows you to identify a specific document belonging to a specific computer that you wish to access. URLs are hierarchical so that the first part refers to the particular website, for example www.bcs.org.uk, but additional identifiers can specify lower level components, for example www.bcs.org.uk/code_of_conduct.

> Originally URLs where called Universal Resource Identifiers (URIs).

Berners-Lee also created the first web-browser and the first web-server (info.cern.ch). The platform that these were created on was the NeXT machine – an interesting choice, but not exactly a mainstream platform. But in one way this was itself making an important point. Berners-Lee wrote:

> '*What was often difficult for people to understand about the design was that were was nothing else beyond URIs, HTTP and HTML. There was no central computer 'controlling' the web, no single network on which the protocols worked, not even an organization anywhere that "ran" the web. The web was not a physical 'thing' that existed in a certain 'place'. It was a 'space' in which information could exist*'.
>
> Berners-Lee and Fischetti (1999, p. 39)

Technological systems based on networks, which include railways and telephones, increase their value as more people adopt and extend the number of nodes on the system and the terminal points on the network. It is rather like that joke about Bell inventing the first telephone in 1876 but it not really taking off until someone had invented the second one. Thus a major part of the story of the internet is the at first slow but then constantly accelerating adoption of the web, enabled by enthusiasts who implemented the protocols for different types of computers and computer environments.

> The factors governing the diffusion of innovation are discussed in Chapter 4.

Dynamic pages

A web with the characteristics outlined in the previous subsection might be excellent as a way of storing and distributing information, but the static nature of the content that is implied does not support the needs of business applications. Anyone who uses the web now will know that web pages can be dynamic, for example there can be moving images.

If a server machine can retrieve an existing HTML document with static content and send it back to the client that has requested it, then it can cheat and create the HTML 'on the fly' in response to the request. It might do this, for example, by taking the details requested from a conventional database and then converting them to HTML. This is known as **server-side processing** and examples of the software technologies that support this include **Active Server Pages (ASP)** from Microsoft, **Java Server Pages** (JSP) from Sun Microsystems and **PHP**: HyperText Preprocessor.

> 'PHP' is a recursive acronym that stands for 'PHP HyperText Preprocessor'.

Another way of making pages active is by transferring executable code to the client which the browser can then execute. This is the principle behind **Java applets** and **ActiveX** controls that carry out **client-side** processing.

Machine-to-machine communication via the web

Normal communication between a client and a server using the internet is already machine-to-machine communication as the client and server are on two different machines. However, at the client end the assumption is that there is a human being accessing the system via a web-browser. This need for a human being can be restrictive. The users may want to access data from another computer using the web and then update a local computer application with the information extracted. Simply reading the information on one system and then typing it into another – known as 'swivel-chair transfer' – is both tedious and error-prone. The solution to this has been to allow machines to communicate directly over the web via **web services**.

TABLE 1.1   *A fragment of XML*

```
<?xml version="1.0"?>
<subjectRecords>
<subject identifier = '0001'>
<dateOfBirth>
<dobdd>3</dobdd>
<dobmm>4</dobmm>
<dobyyyy>1932</dobyyy>
</dateOfBirth>
<dateOfDeath>
<doddd>3</doddd>
<dodmm>4</dodmm>
<dodyyyy>1932</dodyyy>
</dateOfDeath>
<gender>M</gender>
</subject>
</subjectRecords>
```

One obstacle to be overcome that we have touched upon already is that, where human-readable text is communicated, interpretation – if it is in English or another familiar human language – is not a huge problem. When a computer talks to another computer, arrangements have to be in place to encode and interpret the data transmitted. This can be done using **XML (eXtensible Markup Language)**. This can be seen as an HTML for machines. Its concern is not accurate visual presentation, but what the data actually means. In the section on 'The web' above we had an example where the string '0304193223092003M' held the dates when a person was born and died and their gender. This might be presented in XML using statements like those in Table 1.1.

A template for this data structure could be recorded separately using a recognized notation like a **DTD (Document Type Definition)** or a **XSD (XML Schema Definition)**.

The protocol that allows human-free machine-to-machine communication via the web and using XML is **SOAP (Simple Object Access Protocol)**. In order for a web service to be usable by clients, a document must exist in the **Web Service Description Language (WSDL)** which describes what the service actually does, where it exists and how it is called.

UDDI (Universal Description, Discovery and Integration) provides a mechanism that enables directories of web services to be compiled. These registries might be public and generally available, or private and only identify services accessible by systems belonging to a particular organization.

An example of the use of a web service might be where a computer-based payments-received application has to deal with payments made in different currencies. For accounting purposes, foreign currency amounts have to be converted to sterling values at the current exchange rate applicable when the payment was received. The system could request via the internet a web service provided by a financial institution which could return the current exchange rate. This could automate what could clearly be time-consuming clerical work.

> Introductions to the business aspects of web services can be found in Hagel and Seely Brown (2001), Lim and Wen (2003) and Ray and Ray (2006).

BUSINESS AND ORGANIZATIONAL USE OF THE WEB

Ecommerce, ebusiness and egovernment

At first the public internet and the web were the domain of academics and researchers. This was mainly because the internet had originally been financed by the US government and academic institutions. Commercial email services, such as MCI mail and Compuserve, developed in parallel. In 1989 the linking between the commercial services and the not-for-profit internet was permitted. The internet was privatized in the mid-1990s and commercial use since then has flourished.

Many distinguish between ecommerce and **ebusiness**. **Ecommerce** focuses on the buying and selling of goods and services over the internet. Most commonly this is associated with **B2C (business to consumer)** transactions where businesses, such as www.amazon.co.uk, sell goods to individual consumers. Sales transactions could, however, equally be **B2B (business to business)** where, for instance, one business buys components from a supplier which are then assembled. There is also the possibility of one member of the public selling an item, such as an unwanted piece of furniture, to another member of the public, using the internet – this would be **C2C (consumer to consumer)**. This is the equivalent of the small ad in the local newspaper and like that it is usually facilitated by some third party such as eBay. For completeness one can also mention **P2P (person to person)** where the interaction is personal and social in nature rather than commercial – FriendsReunited might be an example of this.

In the previous main section, which talked about the bad old days, a rather primitive state of affairs was described. However, IT practitioners in the business world did not simply sit on their hands putting up with these problems and waiting for the internet and web to come along. There were many developments in EDI (Electronic Data Interchange) that allowed, for example, British Telecom to invoice electronically utility companies such as Scottish Power for their telephone usage. A general problem was that each EDI link had to be developed individually. This meant that nearly all EDI links were B2B. An initial novelty of the web was therefore to enable B2C transactions. However, this particular focus on B2C was not to remain for long.

Ecommerce is just one element of **ebusiness**, which is the term used to describe the wider use of internet and web technologies in a business environment. For example, many large corporations now require job applications to be submitted electronically. It will be recalled from the section on 'The web' that the origins of the web lie in a desire to share technical information. This need still exists. However, an organization might not want to share its information with the whole world. It might, therefore, use web technologies, such as browsers, to create an **intranet** where access is restricted to a chosen few. These could be all or a subset of their staff, or could include some external users such as their distributors. It has been reported, for example, that at Norwich Union key marketing staff have access via an intranet to thousands of pertinent research documents, presentations and reports (Everett 2005). In this example the information is maintained in a **content management system** which is accessed via an intranet.

As well as businesses, government organizations at both national and local levels are using web technologies to inform and to communicate with the citizens of their country, towns or neighbourhoods – hence - **egovernment**.

Business characteristics of the web

The web (or indeed IT in general) is not the solution to every business problem. However, some particular characteristics of the web can be exploited by business applications and these are listed below.

Global reach

The web can be accessed by millions of people worldwide. This means that local businesses can become global ones (Hilpern 2005). The Shropshire Spice Company, for example, based in the heart of rural England has a website that potentially gives it a global presence (www.shropshire-spice.co.uk). However, even where there is access to the web, there are still many communication barriers, the most obvious of which is language. And overcoming communication barriers does not automatically overcome trade barriers, many of which are initially not visible – such as the different formats for European and American DVDs.

A constraint that is perhaps more important for egovernment than for ebusiness is that the reach of the web is not universal in social terms – those who do not have access to the web are often those who are the poorest. One response to this has been to seek alternative ways of accessing the web, by interactive TV or mobile phone for example.

Time independence

A website can operate all day and all night and every day of the year. Apart from allowing domestic consumers to carry out transactions at their own convenience, this contributes to the global reach of the web applications as differences in time between various parts of the globe and national variations in public holidays should no longer cause major problems.

The network effect

We have already noted that network-based systems such as telephones and the railway become exponentially more valuable as more lines, junctions and end-points are added. When email was first introduced the restricted number of users meant that it could only occasionally be useful, but as the numbers of people with whom you could communicate grew, daily use has become essential if you are to keep in touch with colleagues and friends. This network effect is an important one as it applies to many new IT-based products. For example, the ability to send images by mobile phones needs a similar technology at both ends of the communication. This might have discouraged some early potential adopters of the technology.

Information asymmetry

Say a member of the public wants to trade their current car for a better one and for financial reasons they are limited to second-hand vehicles. Unless they have done some research before they go to a second-hand car dealer, the dealers may be at an advantage as they are likely to have a better knowledge of the going market rates for both the car being sold and the one being sought. This disparity in knowledge is known as **information asymmetry** and it is argued that the web has moved the balance of knowledge in favour of the public as they can now more easily compare prices. There are indeed websites that will carry out the comparison for you, for example www.kelkoo.co.uk. Such a comparison process is particularly effective where the product is standard and the quality well-defined, as when different suppliers are selling a product originally manufactured by a single company. There is another argument that this characteristic of the web makes it difficult to sell higher quality, but higher priced, products.

> Measures can be taken to convey a sense of a product's quality – these will be discussed later under the topic of 'Trust'.

As we will see with the next characteristic, the balance of knowledge has not been tilted irrevocably to the side of the customer.

Automatic data capture

Ecommerce involves a mutual exchange of information between buyer and seller using electronic communication. Thus from the outset information is recorded in the language of computers. This eases subsequent processing by IT systems. To make a payment or to specify a place for delivery a customer will have to identify themselves and this information can then be used for marketing analyses (for example, via **data mining**).

> Data mining is explored further in Chapter 5.

Low cost of access

The cost of using web technologies is relatively low. There are several reasons for this. The original development of the internet was heavily financed by the US government. Many of the early enthusiasts for the web were academics who worked in an environment where the free exchange of knowledge and, by extension, software was seen as a great virtue. The network characteristics we have noted earlier mean that there is always an initial concern to promote a network's use as it is the number of users and nodes that make it valuable. One way of promoting a network is to make sure that it is easy and inexpensive to join. With the odd wobble (when Netscape, for example, threatened to charge) browsers have tended to be made freely available. The large numbers of users also mean the hardware needed is likely to be low in price as mass production techniques can be employed in their manufacture.

Scalability and robustness

We can see from the discussion of the origins of the internet that its distributed architecture makes it possible to deal with growth and also resilient in the case of failure in one part of the system.

> **ACTIVITY 1.3 LIMITATIONS, CONSTRAINTS AND DISADVANTAGES OF THE WEB**
>
> **List what you think might be the limitations, constraints and disadvantages of the web (rather than just the internet).**

Revenue models

Of the many frameworks for categorizing ways of making money from the web, the one described below is based loosely on that of Afuah and Tucci (2003). This focuses on ways of generating income. As will be seen later, there could be other motivations for ebusiness development, such as in particular reducing costs. Our categorization is as follows:

* sales;
* commission or referral;
* subscriptions;
* advertising.

Sales

A website can be used to sell goods and services and the revenue comes from sales. In the case of products that can take an electronic format, such as music, e-books and computer games, the web can also act as a delivery channel – an example of the web enabling **cost reduction**. Electronic delivery may also be of value to the customer – this would be an example of the web generating additional **customer value** which might attract the customer to a particular supplier. Customers might even be willing in some circumstances to pay for this additional value.

ACTIVITY 1.4 SALES THAT DO NOT INVOLVE PHYSICAL DELIVERY

Identify two other types of sale where a physical delivery would not be involved.

The sales category is sometimes sub-divided into **mark-up** and **production**. Mark-up refers to the difference in price between buying and selling products and is the way in which retailers, for example, make money. The products here are made by other people. Amazon is one of the most famous of these websites. With the production or manufacturing model, the originator of the goods uses the website to communicate directly with the final customer. With this model, the company might generate larger revenues, not by increased sales, but by taking profits that would normally go to intermediaries.

Commission and referral

In this case there is a sales transaction as described above. This transaction, however, is enabled by a third party who takes a proportion of the payment as commission. An obvious example of this is eBay.

Referral is a variant of the commission model where income is generated by referring visitors to one website to another. Authors of books who have their own website can encourage visitors who wish to buy their book to 'click through' to a book-selling website such as Amazon. A small payment (a micro-payment) may be made to the referring site.

Subscription-based

The customer pays a fixed price on, say, a monthly basis in return for the use of a service. This is typically the case with internet service providers. The charge is often, but not always, independent of usage. The **utility model** on the other hand works on the same principle as most utility services such as gas and electricity: you pay for actual usage.

Advertising

Where a website is frequently used, the website can charge businesses for their advertisements. One of the key factors in successful advertising is to find ways of ensuring that the advertisement is seen by people who are most likely to be potential customers, while not wasting resources on those who clearly are not. Linking advertisements to search engines where the choice of key words for searching could indicate an interest in a particular topic is one way of targeting advertising.

ACTIVITY 1.5 IDENTIFYING REVENUE STREAMS

In what ways do you think the following websites hope to generate income?

- **www.tesco.com**
- **www.ikea.co.uk**
- **www.guardian.co.uk**

The focus above has been on the primary revenue generators where money generally flows from customers outside the supply chain which provides the goods and services. Within the system there will be entrepreneurs who provide enabling services, such as secure payment services, to those enterprises that make up the supply chain.

SUMMARY AND SOME CONCLUSIONS

In this chapter we have stressed the importance of the interplay between the characteristics of a technology – in this case the web – and the various applications that can exploit it. The innate characteristics of the technology will influence the nature of the exploitation; sometimes a technology will reveal a 'need' that no-one has previously foreseen. At the same time, the way that people choose to use a technology will drive the way that it is developed.

There is sometimes an emphasis on the marketplace as a battleground where individualistic business people fight to gain a competitive advantage over their rivals. While there is obviously some truth in this – indeed most governments have legislation to promote such competition – there is also a need for co-operation to set up the systems that allow the markets to exist in the first place. In many cities some of the most impressive buildings are those built to house the markets and exchanges where commerce takes place or has taken place in the past. Compared to these the internet and web are largely invisible to the crowds thronging the streets, but they are at least the equal of these old structures.

SELF-TEST QUESTIONS

1. Which of the following is an advantage of using data packets to transfer data across a network?

    (a) Increased security from hacking.
    (b) More efficient use of transmission channels.
    (c) A variety of types of data can be enclosed in a data packet.
    (d) The data can be read by a browser.

2. Which of the following is a protocol that governs the way computers send and receive data packets across the internet?

    (a) OSI.
    (b) TCP.
    (c) IP.
    (d) HTTP.

3. Which of the following BEST describes the term 'information asymmetry'?

    (a) The speed of data transmission is faster in one direction than in the other.
    (b) Communication cannot take place in both directions at the same time using the particular channel.
    (c) One party to a transaction is more knowledgeable than the other.
    (d) The same information can be more valuable to some recipients than to others.

4. I buy travel insurance online while purchasing a plane ticket. Which revenue model is LEAST likely to be applicable?

    (a) The sales model.
    (b) The commission model.
    (c) The reference model.
    (d) The utility model.

2 Using the Internet to Generate Competitive Advantage

LEARNING OUTCOMES

When you have completed this chapter you should be able to demonstrate an understanding of the following:

- how businesses generate value;
- how to assess the impact on a business's competitiveness of a proposed business change;
- the special nature of knowledge products;
- generic strategies for dealing with competition.

INTRODUCTION

In the last chapter we looked at how the internet and the World Wide Web offered business opportunities. It was stressed that ebusiness takes IT from being a back office operation and places it at the forefront of a company's relationships with the outside world, in particular those with its customers.

Until quite recently, IT developments in business tended to be justified on the grounds of improved efficiency, that is, carrying out operations in a cheaper and speedier manner. Computerizing the production of bills for customers, for example, can reduce the need for staff effort and also, by shortening the time before a customer receives a bill, get money in more quickly and thus improve an organization's cash flow. However, the advent of ebusiness means that IT developments such as the construction of websites to sell goods and services have to create applications that can be good in other ways, such as, for example, by attracting more customers. Systems have not only to reduce costs, but to do so to a greater extent than those of rival enterprises because this means that goods and services can be sold at more competitive prices.

BUSINESS VALUE

IT applications need to contribute to an enterprise's **business value**. Business value can be seen as what is left when an enterprise's costs are taken away from its income. Where an enterprise has shareholders, over a period of time the value of its shares will tend to reflect the business value it generates.

> 'Business value' is very similar to the idea of profit, but perhaps sounds more respectable.

Suppose that a business that we will call 'Brightmouth PC' survives by retailing personal computers. Say that they can buy PCs for £300 and can sell them for £400 – these numbers are purely made up and have been selected to make the arithmetic easy. Let us also say that the rental for their shop, the salaries for staff and other such costs amount to £50,000 a year. They manage to sell 600 PCs in one year. Their **gross profit** would be the difference between the value of their sales and the expenses that can be identified with each individual sale:

Gross profit = (value of sales) – (cost of goods sold)

In this case it would be (600 × £400) – (600 × £300), that is £60,000. In other words, they make £100 for each PC sold. The £300 that is incurred each time a PC is sold is a **variable cost**. If they were able to sell 700 PCs then the total variable costs would go up by 100 × £300, that is by £30,000. This assumes, of course, that there is no discount when purchasing larger numbers of PCs.

However, there are certain costs that will remain the same, regardless of how many units are sold. These include the cost of renting shop premises, salaries, council tax and so on. These are **fixed costs**. Take these away from the gross profit and we get the **net profit**:

Net profit = (gross profit) – (fixed costs)
This can be restated as:
Net profit = (units sold × (price – cost)) – (fixed costs).
In our example above, this would work out as:
Net profit = (600 × (£400 – £300)) – £50,000
$$= £60,000 – £50,000$$
$$= £10,000$$

From this we can calculate the net profit per item sold as £10,000/600, that is, £16.66.

ACTIVITY 2.1 CALCULATING NET PROFITS

What would happen to the total net profits and the net profit per sale for Brightmouth PC in each of the following circumstances?

(a) The shop was able to negotiate a reduction of £50 a unit in the wholesale price of the PCs they buy from their supplier.

(b) The number of sales in a year is increased to 1,200.

(c) The shop is able to increase the price of the PCs it sells to £500 without losing any sales.

(a), (b) and (c) above illustrate three different ways of increasing profits:

(i)   by cutting costs;
(ii) by increasing the volume of sales;
(iii) by increasing the price of goods sold.

Note that in the case of (b) the net profit per individual item sold increases from £16.66 per item to £58.33 per item, simply by increasing the number of items sold without increasing prices or cutting costs. This is because the fixed cost of £50,000 is spread over 1,200 units rather than 600. This propensity for unit costs to decline as the number of items sold increases is an example of an **economy of scale**. This general effect is illustrated in Figure 2.1.

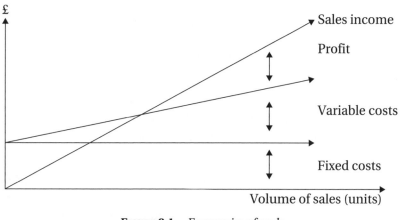

FIGURE 2.1   *Economies of scale*

CUSTOMER VALUE

The problem for Brightmouth PC with the third option above, that of increasing profit by increasing prices, is that their customers are likely to look around to see if there are any other shops that sell PCs at a lower price. In order to justify a higher price they need to offer the customer some additional value for which they are willing to pay.

ACTIVITY 2.2 GENERATING CUSTOMER VALUE

A restaurant can in one way be seen as producing a very basic but very necessary service – the provision of ready-to-eat food that you can consume on the premises and which prevents you from starving. However, the prices charged by restaurants vary hugely. List some of the ways in which a restaurant might provide additional value for which customers might be willing to pay.

PORTER'S FIVE FORCES MODEL

In the example of Brightmouth PC we can see that the freedom of the shop to act to increase its profitability will be constrained by outside forces. For example, reducing the prices at which they purchase PCs would depend on the willingness of the suppliers to accept such a reduction, which they might be very reluctant to do as it would cut their income. On the other hand, the ability to profit from increasing the selling price of PCs to Brightmouth PC's customers would be undermined if the shop's competitors kept their prices low and thus enticed custom away from Brightmouth PC.

The Harvard academic, Michael E. Porter, has devised a **Five Forces model** which explains the likely competitive situation of firms in a business sector. Building on this now well-established model, Porter has subsequently identified ways in which the advent of the internet has had an impact on the competitive forces (Porter 2001) in a business sector (Porter 1980, 1985).

The five competitive forces that Porter has identified are:

(i)   the potential for new entrants to enter a market;
(ii) the rivalry among existing firms;
(iii) the pressure of substitutes;
(iv) the bargaining power of buyers;
(v)   the bargaining power of suppliers.

An imaginary scenario can illustrate the way the Five Forces model might work. Assume that Brightmouth PC are in a position where the demand for their machines is high and they feel that they could sell more if they advertised. They also think that the size of their current shop puts a constraint on the growth of sales. However, the lease on their shop is shortly to run out and their landlords are likely to insist on a large increase in rent. Some initial research shows that alternative high-street sites are likely to be equally or even more expensive. The proprietors of Brightmouth PC are therefore thinking of creating an ecommerce website through which they can sell their wares. They intend to couple this with a move to cheaper premises on an industrial estate on the edge of town. What might be the impact of such moves on their competitive position? An associated question is whether they should focus on consumers who buy PCs for use at home, or on selling to local business and offices. In the former case they would have to generate a large volume of sales with a low average value but in the latter case could have a smaller number of sales which have larger individual values.

> While Brightmouth PC is a small-to-medium enterprise (SME), the issues raised by Five Forces analysis apply equally to larger businesses.

Let us now look at each of the five forces in turn.

Potential for new competitors to enter the industry

This is the ease with which new firms can enter a particular market or industry. If there are high barriers to entry then it will be difficult for newcomers to get a foothold, but existing businesses operating in the field will be more secure. Barriers to entry include the following.

Economies of scale

The idea of economies of scale has been touched upon earlier. If there are a few large businesses each with a substantial share of the market, they will be able to achieve economies of scale and thus be able to offer lower prices to customers than a new entrant which has still to build up its clientele.

Product differentiation

The car manufacturing industry has a number of 'marques' or brands which are well-recognized and which are even supported in some cases by owners' clubs. There is a tendency for at least some motorists to remain loyal to a particular make of car. Where products made by different manufacturers can be clearly identified and brand loyalty has been built up, it can be very expensive for a new player to make an impression by means such as aggressive advertising.

> In the world of computing, Apple computers are a good example of a highly differentiated product.

Capital requirements

Setting up a new business venture usually means having to spend money, not just on advertising, but on other start-up activities such as the acquisition of premises and equipment. The higher these start-up costs, the more difficult it will be for new entrants.

Switching costs

These are the costs that a buyer of goods and services would have to incur in order to switch to a different supplier or product. For example, when someone decides to jettison their old VHS video player and buy a new DVD player, they might also have to purchase DVDs to replace the videos of their favourite films and also transfer any treasured home videos to the new medium. As Brightmouth PC are already in the market they might, for example, try to generate switching costs for existing customers by adding services to the basic sale of equipment, such as, for example, guaranteed maintenance and support or training, which might make established customers reluctant to move to other suppliers.

Access to distribution channels

This is particularly important if you manufacture or assemble products for sale. A successful manufacturer will over the years develop and nurture a distribution network for their goods. There may, in some circumstances, be authorized dealers who not only sell on products but also supply technical advice, support and maintenance services. The existence of such distribution channels can put new entrants at a severe disadvantage.

Cost advantages independent of scale

With the Brightmouth PC scenario, an example of this might be that a rival PC shop in the high street is very well-established and is able to buy rather than rent their shop premises and thus avoid the threat of rent increases. A major advantage for the current players in a market is often learning and experience. Established firms have the experience and skills to do things more efficiently and effectively than new entrants lacking in this know-how. This knowledge might be primarily technical but could also be about things such as the best places to advertise or to obtain components.

> This makes 'knowledge management' an important topic in its own right.

The impact of the internet on industry barriers

The growth of the internet has had a significant impact on the barriers to new entrants in some industries. Use of the internet can overcome distribution barriers by effectively creating an alternative distribution system. The need for local dealers and expensive premises might therefore be reduced. However, many of the additional assets that a web-based enterprise needs, particularly software applications, are, by their nature, easy for competitors to acquire or imitate. For Brightmouth PC there may be a Catch-22 situation: if it is easy for them to set up a web-oriented business, it is just as easy for potential rivals to do so as well.

> A key source here is Michael E. Porter's 'Strategy and the Internet' in *Harvard Business Review* March 2001 – see the references.

Rivalry among existing firms

If the businessesin an industry are intensely competitive then this would be good news for the customer as it would almost certainly lead to lower prices. However, this is probably bad news for the businesses themselves as their profits are likely to be cut as a result.

The following circumstances would encourage rivalry.

A large number of competitors

This could make it difficult for any single competitor to climb to a dominating position. This could happen even with a relatively small number of competitors if they were all equally strong.

Slow growth in an industry

If the market is growing then each competitor can prosper by capturing some of the new customers that are coming forward. Where the market is stagnant or even declining, competitors have to fight for the few customers that are left.

High fixed or storage costs

If fixed costs are high then businesses will be under pressure to sell enough units to cover these fixed costs. It may even be better to sell below cost price in some cases so at to recover at least some of the fixed costs. This is particularly the case if stock is likely to become outdated. For example, Brightmouth PC might want to clear out old models of a particular type of PC if a new, cheaper but more powerful model was about to be released. This will tend to reduce prices and increase price competition.

Lack of differentiation

Where products from different suppliers are indistinguishable and therefore interchangeable, customers are likely to shop around. Buying petrol is a very good example of this.

ACTIVITY 2.3 PRODUCT DIFFERENTIATION

To what extent are the following products differentiated?
(a) Personal computers.
(b) Payroll software packages.
(c) Printer cartridges.
(d) Computer stationery.
(e) Computer games.

Capacity augmented in large increments

In the original Brightmouth PC scenario we identified the possibility of increasing profitability through economies of scale brought about by increased sales. At some point, if Brightmouth PC were able to increase their sales consistently they might get to a point where the existing shop would not be big enough. A rational next step might be to open a new shop. While this would reduce a barrier to expansion, it would also increase fixed costs with the additional costs of a second lease, extra staff and so on. This would be a vulnerable time for the firm, particularly if rivals had also increased their capacity.

Diverse competitors

In some industries there are a range of different types of organizations competing which might have different strengths and weaknesses. Some overseas companies, for example, might have strategic reasons for trying to establish themselves in a particular national market and thus be prepared to sacrifice part of their profits, at least in the short term. All this leads to instability. The growth of internet business has increased these threats.

High exit barriers

Where it is difficult to leave an industry, for example because of the costs of disposing of long-serving employees and specialized equipment, or the existence of long-term contracts, this may create an excess supply of products that will bring down prices.

The effect of the internet on industry rivalry

The general effect of ebusiness has generally been to increase rivalry between competitors and to depress prices. Because the geographical constraints on businesses have been reduced the numbers of competitors that can serve the needs of customers in a particular locality have been increased. By going online, Brightmouth PC have the opportunity to sell over a wider area but will have more competitors for those customers. A big risk for enterprises who have an existing 'bricks-and-mortar' existence is of **cannibalization**, that by moving to a new channel for business they are destroying an old one that may have served them well. Rather than gaining new customers they may simply be transferring old ones to a new, and potentially less profitable, way of doing business.

> A particular case of the risk of cannibalization is where a newspaper produces an online version.

Pressure from substitute products

There is a danger that the product or service that you are selling could be replaced by a different product or service that performs the same function, particularly if the alternative is cheaper or has a better performance. Only a few older people will now know what a slide rule is as they (the slide rules, that is) have been replaced by electronic calculators. Electronic calculators are now themselves threatened by calculator functions on laptop PCs and mobile telephones.

If Brightmouth PC are considering targeting the home user, they might ponder whether the sale of PCs to youngsters might suffer because of the development of specialist games platforms such as the Xbox. Will the development of mobile phone technology mean that people will tend to use their phones to access the web? If nothing else this could put a ceiling on the prices that Brightmouth PC can charge for their products.

An interesting point here is that the threat of substitute products can motivate people who would otherwise be rivals to come together to protect and promote their industry.

Bargaining power of buyers

If the bargaining power of buyers is high this means that they can drive prices down. To illustrate this point recall that earlier it was suggested that Brightmouth PC are debating whether to have a sales strategy which targets home users of PCs or whether to focus on supplying local businesses. In the case of the home market they would have a relatively large number of small customers while in the business market they would expect a smaller number of hopefully bigger customers.

The bargaining power of buyers would be influenced by the following circumstances.

A large proportion of sales go to a relatively small number of buyers

In this scenario, as would be the case if Brightmouth PC went for the office market, the buyers would be in a stronger position to negotiate discounts. The relatively weak position of individual domestic consumers when dealing with large corporations has been recognized by governments who have passed consumer protection laws.

The product is a significant proportion of the buyer's costs

Home buyers of PCs may not be able to negotiate a discount, but because a fair amount of their personal money is at stake they are probably going to be more willing to spend time shopping around for a bargain. Business purchasers for whom the purchase of a single PC is a relatively small item of expenditure compared to say the cost of premises or heavy plant might be happy to buy a more expensive PC if they could do so quickly and with no inconvenience.

Products are undifferentiated

This was discussed earlier. If Brightmouth PC also sells PC-related consumables such as A4 paper then the products from different suppliers are almost identical and I as a consumer can switch suppliers easily to reduce costs.

Low switching costs

This has also been discussed earlier. PCs are essentially the same whoever makes or sells them and I would expect to be able to switch my make of PC without too much difficulty. I would need, however, to be a little cautious that the existing applications that I use currently will still work if, for example, the operating system on the new PC is different. The application software, the operating system and the PC platform form a set of **complementaryproducts** that have all to be acquired to carry out some function. The existence of complementary products can indicate that there is a possible risk of switching costs in changing one of component products.

Buyers earn low profits

We have suggested that if Brightmouth PC sold to large businesses then a large business might not be overly concerned about the price of the occasional PC they might buy compared to other larger out-goings. However, if a business's profits are low, perhaps because it operates in a very competitive field, then it is more likely to be conscious of costs.

Buyers can take over part of the supply chain

If Brightmouth PC target the supply of local large businesses as customers, a concern might be that if a customer feels that the Brightmouth PC prices are too high they might think it worthwhile dealing directly with the manufacturers of the PCs. This would put pressure on Brightmouth PC to keep prices low. Alternatively, part of the Brightmouth PC service might be 'building' the PC, that is, installing the required system software on the initially empty hardware platform. Large users of PCs might use IT support staff to do this for them.

The quality of a product or service is important to the buyer's own products or services

For example, a buyer of PCs might be very dependent on the machines being reliable. A travel agency might need working PCs when taking holiday bookings over the phone. In this case they might be prepared to pay more for Brightmouth PC products if they were able to guarantee to replace any faulty workstation immediately.

The buyer has full information

The concept of **information asymmetry** was introduced in the last chapter. If buyers have access to the selling prices of a wide range of retailers then this puts pressure on suppliers to keep prices low. Clearly the internet makes such price comparisons easier.

The impact of the internet on the power of buyers

Michael E. Porter's analysis emphasizes that the internet tends to increase the power of the buyer. This may be at the cost of product quality as it is easier to sell on price via the internet than to sell on quality.

The power of suppliers

This is to a large extent the mirror image of the buyer's position: where buyers are weak, suppliers will be strong and vice versa. Thus suppliers will be in a strong position when:

- there are a few suppliers dominating an industry;
- there are few or no substitutes for the products they sell;
- individuals are not important customers to the supplier;
- the supplier's products are an important input to the customer's business;
- the supplier's products are differentiated so that the cost of switching to another supplier may be high;
- the supplier can threaten to move into the buyer's area of business.

> ### ACTIVITY 2.4 FIVE FORCES ANALYSIS
>
> **Using the Porter Five Forces framework, what would be Brightmouth PC's relative bargaining strength with regard to the manufacturers from which they purchase their PCs?**

One area where Brightmouth PC might have some bargaining power as a retailer is in their influence over the end-purchaser. If Brightmouth PC can influence purchasers to buy one type of PC rather than another, through their recommendations and advice, then this could encourage the manufacturers to cultivate their relationship with the retailer.

GENERIC STRATEGIES

Generally speaking, there are two basic ways of making money in ebusiness:

(i) by reducing costs so that you can reduce prices – **cost leadership**; or

(ii) by **differentiating your products**, that is, making them special in some way so that people are prepared to pay more.

You can try to do this in either a **broad market** or a **narrow specialist market**.

Cost leadership

In order to compete on price you must be able to do all or some of the following:

- obtain your components and raw materials at low prices;
- assemble and deliver your products and services efficiently;
- get a substantial share of the available market by serving all the major groups of customers;
- supply a wide range of related products.

By doing this you hope to obtain economies of scale which will allow you to keep prices low and thus gain more customers. A danger to be avoided is that low prices must not be at the cost of customers thinking your products and services must be of lower quality than those of your competitors. It is helpful if you can present convincing reasons why you can afford the lower prices in the way that, for example, IKEA does with its emphasis on the customer collecting and assembling the items of furniture that it sells. The use of the internet could be one such justification.

Ebusiness can support economies of scale by widening the reach of your markets – potentially globally – and by removing the costs of having to have a physical presence over a wide geographical area. To reap the full benefits of ebusiness you would probably want to integrate the ecommerce applications which are the 'front-end' of your relationships with the customers with your 'back-end' (or back office) processes such as sales order processing, stock control and management, and purchase ordering. Where these processes have been closely integrated they are often subsumed under the general title of **enterprise resource planning** (ERP). The fact that sales data about your customers is being captured electronically allows you to understand more fully your customers' behaviour and preferences and to target them more precisely through data analyses – or **data mining** – that support **customer relationship management** (CRM). Not only might you focus on using IT to reduce the cost of sales but on the purchasing side you might use **e-procurement** to reduce costs. These topics will be explored further in subsequent chapters.

> ERP is the main subject of Chapter 6.
> CRM and data mining are the discussed further in Chapter 5.

In general, the cost leadership strategy requires a particular, but not exclusive, focus on process.

Product differentiation

Rather than trying to compete on price, you might offer a product that is perceived as being unique in some way that customers might value. This could be through, for example, the design of the product, the technologies used, the quality of the product or service or the after-sales support that is provided. An outstanding example of this approach is Apple, which has clearly differentiated its desktop machines from other personal computers. This approach can build up customer loyalty and thus should be less sensitive to competition on price.

Websites designed to support this approach might, for example, attempt to promote a sense of community among product users through online discussion boards. They might also have frequent downloadable newsletters and reports which provide information about the latest developments in their products and how their products can best be exploited. In general, this strategy requires a particular, but not exclusive, focus on the product.

This is explored further in Chapter 5.

Michael E. Porter (1980) distinguishes further between a differentiation policy which still aspires to having an industry-wide impact and a focus which pays particular attention to just one part of the market such as, for example, a particular locality.

INDUSTRY MATURITY CYCLES

Like any other competitive system – such as that of many sports – the relative strengths and weaknesses of the players will rise and fall over time. This will be very much influenced by the '**maturity**' of the industry.

Early stages

The development of a new technology can lead to the start of a new industry. In the early days of a new industry such expertise and experience that exists will be key factors for a player. The pioneers of the original microcomputers were clearly 'geeks'. In the early days of an innovation it is likely that there will be few expectations about the precise form that a product should take or how it should be built. Different entrepreneurs will pursue different ideas about what features a product will have and how it should be constructed. Early computers, for example, had a bewildering range of different operating systems.

Not all innovations are runaway successes. The important turning point is when customers start to see the product has some value for which they are willing to pay. In the case of microcomputers, the development of personal computing tools – in particular, the word processor and the spreadsheet – attracted purchasers outside the initial small group of electronics hobbyists. The process by which innovations are taken up will be discussed in a Chapter 4. A concern that may emerge at this point is capturing market share. Having a larger number of customers than your rivals means that economies of scale can be made. This would mean you could sell your product more cheaply. On the other hand, if the innovation really takes off, demand could start to outstrip supply.

Middle age

As a new product matures, certain 'rules' will emerge. For example, in the early days of the motor car there were no standards about how the controls should be set out, for example whether a car should be steered or braked using the driver's feet or hands. Over time certain conventions about use have emerged. Similarly, when using new software, particularly web-based applications, users would now expect certain conventions to be followed about the use of toolbars, menus and buttons.

If it looks as if there is money to be made in an industry, then new entrants will be attracted. Some of these will be well-established major concerns diversifying into a new area, such as when IBM started manufacturing PCs. Competition thus starts to become more intense. Some smaller companies will be swallowed up by more successful or larger competitors.

The offerings by different suppliers are likely to converge in terms of the functionality and the features being offered, and competition on price increases.

Maturity and decline

The processes described above will usually lead to a shake-out of smaller and less efficient firms, leaving just a few larger operators as only the most efficient can make a profit. Increasing the scale of operation, however, means that the remaining operators will have invested considerably in the product. This may make it difficult to get out of the market as demand is satiated, and this might lead to overcapacity, that is, supply might start to exceed demand.

ACTIVITY 2.5 THE VALUE OF START-UP COMPANIES

There are stories from the dot com boom period about start-up businesses that were consistently generating losses, but yet were valued very highly in terms of the price of their shares. How might this be explained in the context of the industry maturity life cycle?

Warning: industries and products vary

The above description of an industry maturity life cycle is only a generalization. Each industry based on an innovation has its own story. For instance, booming industries can have periods when overcapacity leads to business crashes – such as the railways in 19th-century Britain and the dot coms in the 21st century – from which recovery can follow.

THE SUSTAINABILITY OF SUCCESS

The picture of the industry maturity cycle shows that many players who pioneer innovative products and services will go out of business as an industry matures. In some cases they will leave the playing field willingly having been bought out by a larger competitor on lucrative terms. David Teece is one of the academics who has noted that the earliest pioneers are often not the ones who reap the benefits of innovation.

What can innovative entrepreneurs do to avoid a premature or unwanted exit from the business sector where they have made an early promising start? According to David Teece (1986), the degree to which innovators are likely to benefit from their pioneering work depends on two interacting factors:

(i) **difficulty of imitation** – the obstacles that prevent others copying an idea;

(ii) **complementary assets** – the things that the entrepreneur needs in order to exploit the innovative idea or product.

Complementary assets might include the functions that would need to be set up to exploit the product or service such as, for example, sales and marketing capabilities, and production and distribution systems. They could include **complementary technologies**: for instance, the hardware and operating system platforms needed to execute an innovative software product. The complementary assets could be generic, as in the case of a distribution system which could be used for a range of different products. The innovative product and the complementary asset could be **co-specialized** where each one could not work without the other: for example, a hardware device might not be able to work without a software driver installed on the computer to which the device is attached. Finally, the innovation and the complementary asset could be **specialized** where one is dependent on the other but not vice versa.

As can be seen from Figure 2.2, the difficulty of imitation and the need for complementary assets interact.

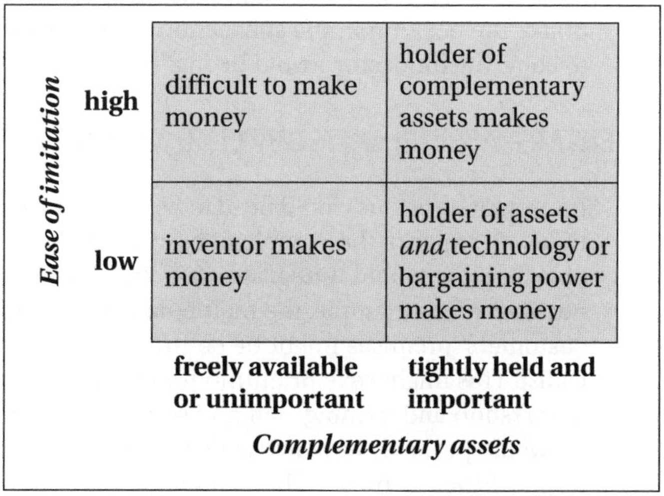

		freely available or unimportant	tightly held and important
Ease of imitation	**high**	difficult to make money	holder of complementary assets makes money
	low	inventor makes money	holder of assets *and* technology or bargaining power makes money

Complementary assets

FIGURE 2.2 *Interaction of ease of imitation and the need for complementary assets*

Ease of imitation and availability of complementary assets

In this situation it would be difficult for the innovator to make money in the longer term from a successful innovation because competitors can copy the idea. Perhaps the best approach here would be a **run** strategy: to attempt to continue to exploit your initial advantage by constantly developing the innovation further and thus keeping one step ahead. This might involve **cannibalization** where new versions of a product make the old versions obsolete.

Ease of imitation and complementary assets tightly held

Earlier, the example of the electronic spreadsheet was used where the development of this tool helped the sales of the microcomputers upon which the spreadsheet ran. Here the microcomputer was a complementary technology whose suppliers benefited from the success of the software tool. Where the product is easy to copy then the innovator's best strategy might be to come to some kind of commercial arrangement with the proprietor of the complementary asset. It might even be best to sell out and let the owners of the complementary asset continue to develop the product in-house.

Difficulty of imitation but availability of complementary assets

Here a **blocking** strategy might be most effective. An aggressive policy of establishing and protecting intellectual property rights over the innovation might be the result.

Difficulty of imitation and complementary assets tightly held

If the same person holds both the rights to the innovation and the complementary assets then they are in a very strong position. Where different people own them, then **teaming up** would be advantageous, but unlike the position in the subsection above, where the innovation is easy to copy, the innovator would be in a stronger position to negotiate.

COMPLEMENTARY ASSETS: OUTSOURCING VERSUS INTEGRATION

Important decisions would need to be made by a concern like Brightmouth PC about which of the 'complementary assets' needed to meet its ebusiness objectives it would **integrate** into the business and which it would **outsource**. For example, the maintenance of PC equipment at its business customers' premises might be contracted out to a self-employed IT specialist. This might save Brightmouth PC the money involved in setting up a workshop and training staff and so on. On the other hand, Brightmouth PC would probably have less control over the specialist outside the specific terms of their contract. The contractor, for example, would probably not see their visits to the premises of customers as an opportunity to sell more IT equipment. This is a relatively simple example, but decisions about what to integrate and what to outsource would be a major influence on the character of a commercial organization.

Many have hailed ebusiness as bringing about a world of virtual organizations where goods and services are delivered to the client through a network of interacting but independent business units which co-ordinate their activities through the internet. The way that such value chains can be supported by the internet will be the main topic of the next chapter.

RESOURCE-BASED VIEWPOINTS

In this chapter the focus has been on the environment in which the business operates. The approach has generally been to find those places where the firm can win custom and profits. Those activities which do not add to profits can be farmed out or dropped altogether. Some business researchers (e.g. Hamel and Prahalad 1989, Prahalad and Hamel 1990) have argued that this cannot fully explain why some businesses have done so well. They point to businesses such as Honda, which was originally a maker of 50cc motor bikes. Over the years the company has developed new products in areas as diverse as lawn-mowers, outboard motors and cars. In the case of cars, Honda now challenges the global position of General Motors. Honda's original competitive strength was access to cheap labour, but that initial advantage cannot explain Honda's progress. Hamel and Prahalad argue that Honda and other successful innovators have been able to grow **core competencies**, expertise in technologies that can be adapted and incorporated into a number of what might appear to the outsider to be very different products. Thus Canon's competencies in optics, imaging and microprocessor controls have allowed it to enter fields as varied as photocopiers, laser printers, cameras and document scanners.

One way in which core competencies can be lost is through outsourcing a key activity or stopping doing business in a particular market altogether. While in some cases the financial pressures for doing this are strong, the business should weigh this against the possibility of future benefits that might come from developing new products using expertise that may have been built up over many years. In the very small example of Brightmouth PC, contracting out maintenance might mean, for example, that the company would not be able to benefit from future demands for the maintenance of new types of office equipment. It would be difficult for them to expand into new areas of maintenance and support because their staff would no longer have direct involvement in these types of activity. They would not be able to identify and implement new approaches to maintenance that might cut costs or improve customer service.

Some have distinguished between core competencies and **capabilities** (e.g. Stalk et al. 1992). Core competencies focus on the expertise needed to develop and bring to the market new products. 'Capability', it is suggested, refers not so much to technical expertise, but to the ability to carry out particular business processes effectively. For example, in the US, Wal-Mart's distribution systems – which among other things employ a 'cross-docking' technique that enables deliveries from suppliers to Wal-Mart warehouses to be broken down and re-shipped to stores without having to be stored in the warehouse for a long period – have been identified as one such capability.

33

The growth of core capabilities can be seen as part of a broader process of **organizational learning**. There has been activity, among researchers, academics and others, to develop the idea of **knowledge management**. Two broad approaches have emerged. One focuses on the human aspects, and examines practices such as staff development, skills audits and job rotation. Another line of attack is to try to identify technologies that might be able to help internal knowledge transfer. The development of **intranets** and **content management systems** are two examples of efforts in this direction.

SELF-TEST QUESTIONS

1. A product costs £50 a unit to assemble and can be sold at £60 a unit. Fixed costs are £600 a year. 250 units are sold. What would be the gross profit?

   (a) £10.
   (b) £15,000.
   (c) £1,900.
   (d) £2,500.

2. According to Porter, which one of the following would favour the entry of new competitors to an industrial sector?

   (a) High switching costs.
   (b) Low economies of scale.
   (c) High product differentiation.
   (d) High capital requirements.

3. According to Porter, which one of the following strengthens the ability of the supplier to increase prices?

   (a) The cost of the product is a significant proportion of the buyer's costs.
   (b) Product differentiation is high.
   (c) Switching costs are low.
   (d) Buyers' profits are low.

4. Which of the following best describes the process of 'cannibalization'?

   (a) A supplier making changes to a product or service so that previous products and services of the supplier become obsolete.
   (b) Taking components of an existing product and using them to build a new product.
   (c) Buying up smaller competitors.
   (d) Bringing the production of some components in-house.

5. You have developed a new service which can be delivered over the internet and is likely to be popular with the public. It is, however, likely to be easy to copy by competitors. It also needs extensive complementary assets to market and administer which requires specialist skills. Which of the following is most likely to be the best strategy?

   (a) Teaming up with a holder of the complementary assets.
   (b) Blocking imitation by competitors.
   (c) Trying to keep ahead of the competitors by constant innovation.
   (d) Outsourcing the delivery of the new service to a third party.

3 The Value Chain and the Internet

LEARNING OUTCOMES

When you have completed this chapter you should be able to demonstrate an understanding of the following:

- supply chains and supply chain management;
- value models;
- disintermediation and re-intermediation;
- identifying core competences and consideration of outsourcing non-core activities.

INTRODUCTION

In Chapter 2, the small-scale business used as an example, Brightmouth PC, was deliberately presented as a business whose structure and situation in the world were simple and easy to grasp.

In this chapter a broader view is taken of the business as a player in a larger network of businesses. Each **first-tier supplier** of Brightmouth PC would be itself a business. It would have its own, **second-tier**, suppliers of goods and services, which in turn would have their own, **third-tier**, suppliers and so on. On the sales side, Brightmouth PC's own customers could themselves be businesses and have their own customers. These various supplier-customer relationships build up into a complex business network. When we as consumers buy an item of clothing, a household appliance or some other item in a department store we pay not just the store but also indirectly for the sub-products and services that contributed to the existence in the right place of the item we have bought.

> First tier means the supplier delivers directly to the business. Second tier suppliers supply first tier suppliers and so on.

This network of processes and businesses (see Figure 3.1) contributing to the item that we take home is the **supply chain** – some argue that 'supply tree' would be more accurate as many separate diverging branches would be found as you traced back the supply chain. In the last chapter the concept of **customer value** was introduced. The key element of this was the price that a customer would be willing to pay. Restaurants as an example illustrated that many things might influence how much we would be happy to pay for a meal, many of which might have little to do with the actual food. Each of these things can be said to add to customer value.

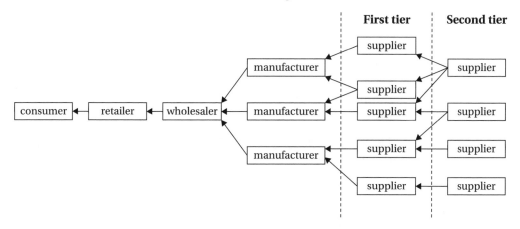

FIGURE 3.1   *An example of a supply chain*

In the case of an item of clothing sold in a department store, at some point workers, probably in a distant land, generated value by converting thread into cloth. Other workers working for a different company might have added further value by dying the cloth, and other workers in a different factory converted the cloth into the actual garment. Notoriously the actual garment makers usually receive only a small share of the final sale price. Others will have generated more value through such things as contributing fashionable design, attractive packaging and transporting the goods to a locality where buyers who can afford them can see and buy them.

These interlinked activities that each add to the value of the final products are collectively called a **value chain**. Unlike the supply chain these activities are not limited to processes that physically take inputs and make them into outputs. Also some value can be added after a product is in the hands of the purchaser, such as, for example, the maintenance of cars.

VALUE CHAIN MODELS

Porter's value chain model

The challenge for all functions within an organization – including IT – is to show how they contribute to value. Michael E. Porter (1985) has devised a widely used model that identifies the generic activities that contribute to customer value.

The key activities are as follows.

- **Inward logistics** are needed to obtain, store and supply to the right location the raw materials, components and data needed by the operations process.
- **Operations** turn the inputs from the inward logistics activities into outputs.

37

- **Outward logistics** receive the finished goods and distribute them to customers as required.
- **Marketing and sales** include activities that identify potential customers and their needs, and induce them to buy the goods and services produced by the business.
- **Services** are activities that enhance the value of the product when it has been acquired by the customer, for example by training in its use, or help to sustain its value, for example by maintenance.

These key areas of activity are enabled and supported by **secondary** or **support** activities that include the following.

- **Procurement:** finding the best sources of the materials, components and services needed by the business to make its products.

> Recall that value can be increased by reducing costs.

- **Technology development:** this includes research, development and change management aimed at improving existing products and developing new ones and also enhancing processes.
- **Human resource management:** recruiting, hiring, training, developing and paying staff.
- **Firm infrastructure:** this covers the remaining activities such as general management, planning, premises management, IT infrastructure management, financial and legal services.

ACTIVITY 3.1 ADDING VALUE

Identify the type of activity in the Porter value chain model that each of the following would enhance.

(a) **Radio frequency identification (RFID) tags put on pallets and cases of components when shipped to a business by a supplier and also used by the business to locate components in its storerooms.**

(b) **A self-service function that allows employees to upgrade directly details such as home addresses and bank details that are held by their employer on a human resources system.**

(c) **A self-service system in a supermarket that allows customers to check out baskets of purchases and make payments without using a cashier.**

(d) **Electronic price signs on shelf edges in a supermarket that can be updated by a central system at the local branch.**

(e) **Use of internet-enabled reverse auctions – where the lowest bid wins – to find the cheapest source of office materials such as office stationery.**

Secondary activities do not generate value directly but maintain the viability and enhance the effectiveness of primary activities. Thus any proposals for IT developments need to demonstrate that they enable the secondary and primary activities to generate additional value either by reducing costs, by enriching the products so that customers are willing to pay for them, or by attracting more sales. For example, in a financial services company there was a proposal to introduce an elearning application which would allow customer advisers to learn about the detailed specifications of new and modified financial services products while sitting at their workstations. The proposal justified the development on the grounds that it saved the costs of conventional training events and made better use of advisers' time. It also made the interactions with customers more effective as the advisers would be better informed about the company's products and sales might increase as a result. Thus **technology development** would help to cut the costs of the **human resource management** activity of training, and also make the primary activity of **marketing and sales** more effective.

> ### ACTIVITY 3.2 APPLYING THE VALUE CHAIN MODEL TO A BANK
>
> **A bank provides current accounts for its customers. Customers can deposit and withdraw money. They can earn interest on the money in their account, but have to pay interest on their overdrafts. The bank uses a proportion of the money in the current accounts to make loans on which interest is charged.**
>
> **How does this business application map onto the Porter value chain?**

The basic model of the value chain that closely reflects the supply chain is less useful when analysing some types of business. The model can clearly be applied to manufacturing concerns but in the UK this is a relatively small sector compared to, for example, financial services. The first obvious limitation is that the value chain is difficult, if not impossible, to apply to not-for-profit organizations such as publicly run schools and hospitals where the concept of 'customer value' is hard to apply.

> This is not to say they do not give 'customers' value, but that it is hard to put a precise financial figure on it.

It is argued that the model needs to be modified where a business is concerned with product development – which includes software and other IT development. This would involve some kind of development life cycle, a concept familiar to information systems (IS) practitioners and software engineers. Such development processes are likely to be treated as a project, a unique process using transient resources, rather than as a continuous process.

The balance between the different primary and secondary activities will, in any case, depend on the type of business. 'Operation'-type activities in some businesses will be negligible. A company that sells insurance might have developed a set of standard products. When a policy is sold, the production of the individual policy is relatively straightforward: most of the work will come from the 'services' element, collecting premiums and dealing with claims.

With **knowledge-based** products, such as books, records and films, the initial development costs are very high but the cost of the operation of creating each additional copy of the product is very low. This characteristic is magnified where products can be held digitally and can thus be delivered to consumers over the web.

Organizational technologies

Charles Stabell and Øystein Fjeldstad (1998) have argued that the under-standing and application of the concepts of value chains and value models can be improved if they are applied with an awareness of the different types of **organizational technologies** that exist. J.D. Thompson (2003) has suggested that organizations tend to conform to three major configurations.

(i) **Long-linked technology.** Here value is created by transforming inputs into products. Assembly-line manufacturing is a prime example. This maps easily to the basic Porter value chain model.

(ii) **Intensive technology.** With this configuration, customers bring problems which they wish to have solved. Different problems will require different solutions so the processes that the organization will carry out will vary between customers. Firms that carry out pro-fessional services in areas such as medicine and health, law, finance, design and engineering would be prime examples. Stabell and Fjeldstad suggest a variation on the basic value chain model that they call the **value shop** which we will discuss in a little more detail below.

(iii) **Mediating technology.** The organizational configuration is designed to bring together clients or customers who wish to transact some type of business. Often it will be clients who are buyers and sellers, but this is not necessarily so as with a telephone network. As in the case of intensive technologies, Stabell and Fjeldstad suggest a specific value model for this configuration – **value networks**.

Long-linked technology and the value chain

While the Porter value chain can be conveniently mapped onto the Thompson long-linked technology model, the two are different. A value chain activity such as inward logistics could be carried out by a number of different physical units within a business. A particular unit could also carry out more than one type of value chain activity.

It can also be argued that the long-linked technology model was originally devised to apply in organizations where processes were arranged into sequences of interrelated physical activities that passed information and physical materials between each other – the classic example of this being the assembly line. Sub-divisions might arise because of the innate nature of the physical processes, or because different skills were needed at different stages or even because of the different geographical location.

The computers used in organizations in the 1960s and 1970s also contributed to this approach as real-time communication with a computer was rare and most computer processing was done on batches of documents which were completed by clerks in offices and were then passed to data centres for processing. As a result, many of the conventional systems analysis techniques, particularly the use of workflow and data flow diagrams, reflect this way of organizing work.

Proponents of **business process re-engineering** (BPR) – see Michael Hammer and James Champy (1993) – would argue that administrative processes that involve documents being passed from one department to another for different elements of processing can, with modern technologies, be re-engineered so that the different activities can be done as a single process in one place at one point in time. This process is sometimes called **hubbing**. One small example of this is a company that deals with motor insurance. As part of its claims process the claims clerk had to send details of each claim to a second department in order to schedule when an inspector could look at the damage to the vehicle. A new computer system gave the clerks direct access to the inspection schedules so that they could book the inspections directly.

A limitation on the conventional analysis techniques is that the analysts work for a particular organization and are trying to design systems that work within that organization. While this is only to be expected, we will see that widening the analysis to consider the complementary processes in other organizations – while challenging – can bring significant benefits.

The value shop

If your car breaks down on the highway and you call out one of the breakdown services such as the AA or the RAC, your situation is that you have a problem and you are calling upon an expert to provide a solution. The precise nature of the cause of the problem is not known at the outset and a range of solutions depending on the nature of the cause is available. In the case of a mechanical fault in a motor vehicle, the nature of the cause of the breakdown is likely to be relatively straightforward. In other cases where help is sought there may be a range of contributory causes and a number of different specialisms may need to be called upon.

The classic definition of a 'problem' is the difference between an existing state and a desired one, for example between your car not working and it working. The problem, however, could be the difference between the status quo and the exploitation of a perceived opportunity.

Stabell and Fjeldstad see the key activities in the value shop model as follows.

- **Problem-finding.** From the point of view of the service provider this involves being notified of the request for help and collecting information about the nature of the problem.
- **Problem-solving.** The cause of the problem is diagnosed and one or more possible solutions are identified.
- **Solution selection.** Different solutions to the same problem may have different characteristics: for example an immediate but temporary solution, as opposed to a more time-consuming but longer-lasting one. Different solutions will also have different costs. A choice would usually be made in consultation with the client.
- **Solution execution.** The chosen remedial actions are carried out.
- **Solution evaluation.** The outcome from the remedial actions would need to be monitored and adjustments made where needed. For example, there may be more than one cause of a malfunction and the removal of one cause may bring others to light.

While these activities may differ from those of the classic Porter model, the supporting secondary activities are similar. Many organizations could carry out both value chain and value shop activities, as when an organization builds new products and repairs old ones.

Value networks

The core business of the value network is to bring together people who wish to form some kind of relationship, for example potential buyers and sellers. Estate agents, for instance, are in the business of bringing together potential buyers and sellers of houses and other property. In the world of the internet, C2C services such as eBay are examples of value networks. Some examples suggested by Stabell and Fjeldstad are not so obvious. They suggest, for instance, that insurance companies act as value networks as they bring together people willing to pool resources which can be called upon when a member of the network suffers a particular kind of loss.

A key contributor to the success of such networks is their size. The more potential sellers there are, the more choice there is for a buyer. The more potential buyers, the more chance there is of a sale at a reasonable price for the seller. This need for **critical mass** means that the start-up of such a network can be a period of uncertainty and risk.

ACTIVITY 3.3 VALUE CHAINS, SHOPS AND NETWORKS

Classify each of the following businesses as either a value chain, value shop or value network:

(a) An insurance broker.

(b) A used car dealer.

(c) An amateur football club.

(d) A rock star.

DISAGGREGATION OF BUSINESS ACTIVITIES

A good source on disaggregation is Evans and Wurster (2000). It is unlikely that a single value model could be mapped onto any substantial business organization. Businesses can appear to be fairly random collections of business operations each of which could have its own business model. Take the example of a car dealership which is a local franchise of a large car manufacturer. The business has a showroom where new vehicles are sold, workshops where maintenance and repairs are carried out and a spare parts department. In addition to selling new cars it sells second-hand cars that have been part-exchanged by their owners for new models.

Such aggregations of different functions might be justified on the grounds of the **synergies** between them. For example, repairs to cars sold by the franchise would be free during the warranty period and so having a repair facility associated with the sales function is convenient. Repair and maintenance would need to have access to spare parts so having that department close at hand is also clearly convenient, and the second-hand sales unit can be seen to dove-tail with new sales as it can be used to dispose of second-hand cars that have been bought as part-exchange deals. A further justification could be the synergies generated by shared expertise and knowledge about the particular marque of cars. Customer loyalty might also be nurtured as a purchaser of a car might keep bringing it back for servicing and then eventually part-exchange it for a new vehicle.

> In this context 'synergy' means extra value generated by different systems working together.

Major competition will come from the dealers for other leading marques of cars who might compete with all the dealership's activities. However, other competitors might attack just one valuable part of the business. For example, a local business which specializes in second-hand car sales and has a large number of vehicles of all makes could be a powerful competitor in just that area.

Bearing in mind the competitive factors explored in the last chapter, some parts of the business may be in a better competitive position than others. Car sales will have to compete with those of other manufacturers and as a result prices will be relatively low. However, once you have bought a car from the dealer you may be effectively locked into having to buy spare parts from them at inflated prices.

Thus business can be **deconstructed** or **disaggregated** into separate functions or **profit centres**. Decisions can be made about whether to retain those functions in-house or to move them outside the organization.

Even when operationally the business seems to be a single coherent functional unit, the outputs from the unit can often be broken down into products and services that are consumed by different market segments. Thus some new cars may be sold to individual private customers who pay with their own money, while other sales are to businesses with fleets of cars. Demand and competition will vary from one segment to another in the market and a decision could be made to focus exclusively on one segment.

In some cases the business will still need the services of a particular function, but still find it beneficial to **outsource** the service so that it is provided to the business from outside the company. IS and IT practitioners will know – perhaps only too well – that this is very common with IS and IT services. Several options exist for the transition to external sourcing, for example the internal unit could simply be dissolved, the unit could still exist but its ownership be transferred, or a separate corporate entity could be set up whose shares are partly or wholly owned by the parent company. A powerful incentive for outsourcing has been that this makes it easy for labour-intensive operations to be transferred to developing countries where wages are lower – this is known as **off-shoring**.

> A process whereby the cost of carrying out a function internally as compared to it being carried out externally is a form of **benchmarking**.

One example of where a company has set up one of its functional units as a separate trading entity has been Eastman Chemical Company spinning off its logistics operation into a separate company, Cendian (Yen et al. 2004). Because Cendian had once been part of Eastman its communication channels with Eastman were very well integrated and to a large extent automated. Cendian, however, can also generate revenues by providing chemical logistics services to other companies.

This flexibility in using the services of external companies to carry some functions while retaining those that generate most customer value gives great advantages to new entrants by reducing some of the barriers to a new market.

An example of how a new entrant can attack a vulnerable component of an existing business is the case of small advertisements in newspapers. A newspaper can be seen as conglomeration of different products and services. For some customers the primary value of a newspaper could be as a source of information about the results of sports events, for others as a guide to what is on television or on at the local cinemas, and so on. A particular area of interest for some will be the small advertisements for jobs and cars. This motivates some people to buy the newspaper. It would also be a distinct and substantial source of revenue which subsidizes and enables other content. It is thus vulnerable to attack from publications which might specialize exclusively in advertisements for items such as motor vehicles. These might have no editorial content, but be given away for free. An easier step for someone trying to enter this market would be to set up a website. Clearly, the proportion of the target audience who actually have web access would need to be assessed. Website maintenance would probably be less costly than producing regular print publications and web content can be more current than print as it can be updated on a continuing basis. If successful, web-based small advertisements could undermine the viability of many local papers. Newspaper proprietors are not going to stand idly by with such a threat and many are forestalling web-based rivals by setting up websites themselves. This kind of development by incumbents in a particular market will be explored further in the next section.

We can summarize the argument of this section as follows. Established businesses need to be able to 'deconstruct' their operations and services into their value-adding component activities and examine each one carefully. They must judge whether it is still worthwhile to keep the activity within the core organization or whether to discontinue the activity and depend on outside providers. They must also identify actual and potential external competition – which could well be web-based – that could attack component business activities. A key consideration in such decision-making is the value that is generated by each component of the business.

ACTIVITY 3.4 DISAGGREGATING THE ACTIVITIES OF A UNIVERSITY

Assume a university can be treated as a business.
- Disaggregate the activities of a university into component value creating units.
- Identify external organizations (apart from other universities) that currently exist that could take over those functions. In each case state whether this would be as a competitor or as an outsourcer.
- Are there any core functions that in your view could not be outsourced?

THE DOWNSTREAM VALUE CHAIN

We are now going to look at how the rise of internet-based B2C applications can affect the relationship between a supplier and the final customer.

Disintermediation

A new entrant into a market can gain advantages over incumbent retailers by direct sales customers. This strategy predates the internet as the use of mail order and telesales has been well-established for many years. Thus an insurance company can reduce costs by selling directly to customers via a call centre. A travel company can by-pass travel agents and let holiday-makers book holidays online.

This removal of an intermediary between the suppler and customer is known as **disintermediation** (see Figure 3.2). Dell's computer sales, for example, are direct to the customers and local retailers like Brightmouth PC are disintermediated. This is easier for new entrants who have no existing relationship with intermediaries.

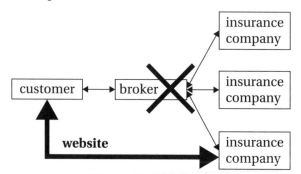

FIGURE 3.2 *Disintermediation: the customer deals directly with the insurance company via the website, rather than through the broker*

Intermediaries such as travel agents and insurance brokers sell the products of a range of suppliers. They can add value by providing information about different products, highlighting their differences and offering practical advice. Where the long-term consequences of a purchase are significant, as with a pension plan, customers are more likely to want such advice. In this case, local brokers or agents may have considerable influence over the purchasing decisions of customers.

There are at least two possible consequences. Intermediaries may focus on the more complex and therefore usually higher value business transactions and give up the simpler and cheaper transactions which may be more amenable to purchase over the internet. Internet businesses may take up this challenge by designing interactive websites that go some way to offering the information and advice that a personal intermediary offers. Dell's website, for example, has very detailed product descriptions and standard recommended configurations for different types of use.

An alternative to disintermediation is to use IT to create a closer relationship between the supplier and the intermediary. At least one financial services company has introduced an XML-based new business tracking application that can be used by insurance brokers to input details of new business and then track its progress through the system. The flexibility provided by XML and web service technology means that the intermediaries can either buy certain off-the-shelf (OTS) packages which provide the links or develop their own application to access the information. The data formats used in the XML-based application are industry standards, so the same system can potentially be used to deal with different providers of financial products. Intermediaries therefore may have fewer worries about adoption of the application reducing their competitive advantages by locking them into a single provider.

> XML stands for eXtensible Markup Language. Its use facilitates the transfer of data between systems. This and web services were discussed in Chapter 1.

In some cases the intermediary may have a closer, contractual, relationship with the supplier. Such is the case with car dealerships. Manufacturers are very dependent on the local dealerships in a number of ways, one of which is that most purchasers want to be able to test-drive a car before purchase. It would, in these circumstances, be very difficult for the manufacturer to appear to be undermining local dealers by introducing direct sales of vehicles through the web.

A particular case of this is with popular high street names such as the Body Shop where most local branches are locally owned as franchises, and here direct sales would clearly be seen as being against the interests of the local investors.

Where the local branches are owned by the main retailer, direct sales could simply have the effect of moving some sales that would have been made in its shops to the internet – this is an example of **channel conflict**. Where a particular channel is under threat from competitors a business might decide to accept the fact that the development of the new channel will be at the expense of an existing one. This is another example of cannibalization where a new development damages the existing assets of a business, as where a new product makes an existing one obsolescent. A previous example of this was a newspaper that creates a small-advertisements website. This could take some business away from paper-based advertisements, but for some sellers of items having an advertisement in both paper and electronic format might be attractive. This could make the multi-channel medium better value than the offering of an internet-only competitor.

Web navigators and re-intermediation

The use of the web to remove intermediaries and to drive down prices for the customer is a good thing for the consumer at large, especially as the web can present information about a large number of choices. The problem is often how a prospective buyer selects between the often bewildering range of products and services. While giving consumers more choice should bring more sales – there is more chance that they find what they want – sometimes too much choice leads to confusion and deters a purchase (see Gladwell 2006, p. 142).

ACTIVITY 3.5 MAKING A PURCHASE

Think about some major purchases that you have made recently, perhaps a car. How did you go about finding out about the products available and how did you go about your final selection. Try to think about more than one example. Did you always use the same approach? If not, why not?

The behaviour of purchasers will differ between individuals. However, some broad scenarios might be imagined. Where a particular purchase is an infrequent one then some kind of search will need to be done by the prospective purchaser. The search is likely, at least initially, to be 'top-down'. Say you want to buy a new washing machine, then firstly you may want to remind yourself of the major makes and the locations where you can buy them. This search to generate a basic list of options will use simple criteria and you will probably feel happier if you know that your search is fairly comprehensive – for example, that you have not missed a shop which is just around the corner. Your next step would probably be to 'drill down' – to pick a few of the more promising possibilities and investigate them individually. This will mean actually visiting the shop in most cases. When you investigate one possibility, you may find that it cannot meet one of your requirements – perhaps in the case of the washing machine to wash all kit for the first, second, third and fourth teams of your local rugby club – and you have to go back to your initial list and try another option. Once you find a washing machine that meets your requirements then you are likely to spend some time, but not too much, checking out even cheaper or better machines: your search strategy is like to be **satisficing**, searching for the good enough, not an **optimal** strategy which attempts to seek out the very best.

The underlying model for this scenario suggests a top-level search for a limited amount of information about a wide range of options, followed by drilling down to get more information about individual prospects. There will be a certain amount of movement between the two levels, which might involve some refinement of the search criteria.

If you use the internet to carry out some of the processes of selecting a product you will probably use some intermediary to start off your search, even if it is a very generalized one like Google. For certain types of search you would probably use a specialist site such as Amazon for book titles, Expedia or Travelocity for air travel, uSwitch (which was sold in March 2006 for £210 million – Brignall 2006b) for gas and electricity, and moneysupermarket.com or Confused.com for insurance. Such websites are examples of **re-intermediation** (see Figure 3.3), the introduction of new intermediaries between the user and the supplier. They are examples of **navigators**, websites that are designed to help web users to find their way around the internet. They can be seen as a particular type of value network – recall the subsection on 'Value networks'. Note that best buy websites usually get commission for recommendation and so may not be entirely impartial (Brignall 2006b).

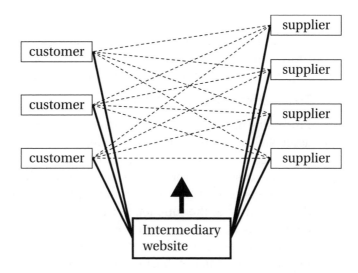

FIGURE 3.3   *Re-intermediation: customers are helped in their choice of supplier by an intermediary website*

In that subsection, it was noted that size was important in the sense that the greater the coverage, the greater the chance of the users getting the full information they need. Where the number of relevant data subjects is high – in the case of book titles this will be in the millions – then once a navigator gets a substantial lead over its competitors, it tends to achieve a **critical mass** which means that it becomes the navigator of choice and the remainder are in danger of fading away. As noted earlier, value networks which are attempting to build up coverage are particularly vulnerable. It is perhaps significant that Amazon was able to get a good start, not by painstakingly building up its initial portfolio of books but by using existing trade databases.

It has been argued by Chris Anderson (2006) that the ease with which relatively obscure products, say less current and less fashionable books or music recordings, can now be located and purchased has radically changed the nature of the market place. As a crude rule of thumb, retailers currently make 80 per cent of their sales from the top-selling 20 per cent of their product lines. The easier access to 'back catalogue' items – the 'golden oldies' – facilitated by internet navigators means that over time these items will generate a larger proportion of sales.

Information scientists point out that the number of responses to a search engine request is not the only measurement of the quality of search. The number of hits has to be balanced against the proportion which are actually relevant and useful, that is **retrieval** effectiveness has to be weighed against the **precision** of the items retrieved.

In a particular domain of interest, access to a smaller database of more focused and precise details may be preferable to being overwhelmed with items the relevance of which is often very mysterious. For example, if you were looking for job vacancies in a very specialist field, the job advertisements in the trade paper or the website of the professional body for that group of specialists are likely to be more useful than entries in more generalized situations vacant databases.

Transaction cost versus trust

Processing orders online will be attractive to many businesses as the costs associated with automated processing will be so much lower than with processes that involve costly human beings.

Before customers can carry out an on online transaction, they have actually got to find their way to the supplier's website. They also need a degree of trust in the supplier. Trust is enhanced by social interaction. We are more likely to trust people we know and also more likely as traders to treat people we know with more consideration – especially if they know our mother as well. Internet business transactions are clearly at a disadvantage here. Thus internet businesses will usually make a conscious effort to build up trust. Most successful internet traders have a well-publicized and liberal returns policy so that prospective purchasers will be reassured about returning an item if is not what they expected. Another way of building trust and confidence is through **affiliation** to an existing well-known and respected institution.

> Bad experiences might discourage ecommerce in general – hence there has been some governmental intervention – see Chapter 4.

There is also the question of the degree to which a supplier can trust a customer, particularly their credit-worthiness. Given the relative anonymity of the purchasers, the answer appears to be 'not a lot'. Payments for goods are usually made up-front, typically by credit card so that the risk of non-payment is outsourced to the credit card company. Payment before delivery is a particular bonus for traders as the early receipt of money reduces the need for working capital to pay their suppliers.

The establishment and maintenance of customer relationship will be explored further in Chapter 5.

THE UPSTREAM SUPPLY CHAIN

We are now going to look at the situation where the business is itself the customer of organizations that supply it with goods and services.

Joint development

As we will see, some relationships between a business and its suppliers will be closer and more important than others. While some of the materials and services that a business needs are straightforward commodities and utility services with clear and generally accepted quality standards, some requirements, especially for high-technology firms, are going to be unique and also key to the company's on-going operation. In these cases, a close relationship between the client and supplier will need to be forged, especially if business transactions of considerable value are involved.

Chris Ibbott of Vodafone has described such a relationship between his company and Ericsson (Ibbott and O'Keefe 2004). Vodafone, which has its base in Newbury in the UK, is a very big mobile network operator. It operates in 28 countries around the world. This is often through local firms which may be part-owned by Vodaphone. Ericsson provides the cellular network used by Vodafone. It also makes the mobile handsets needed to access Vodafone services. One problem in the past has been that the local subsidiaries tended to have their own contracts with Ericsson. Subsidiaries of Vodaphone in different countries tended to have different standards and to duplicate some activities such as testing. In 1998 Vodafone and Ericsson agreed to integrate their supply chains more closely across the world. They set up joint groups to work on these problems. They looked at things like the establishment of technical specifications for new products and worldwide standards for Vodafone networks. To help this work the two firms set up an 'eRelationship', a shared extranet which contained working documents, product descriptions, order configuration tools and software updates.

It is interesting that, in order to formalize and better integrate its relationship with Ericsson, Vodafone had to integrate the operations of its own subsidiaries so that they acted more consistently across the globe. Vodafone would have improved its bargaining power by consolidating its purchasing decisions. This is typical of many organizations where different units make their own purchases of goods and services from different suppliers. Savings can be made by bringing these purchases together and negotiating discount on larger orders.

Dedicated staff can also focus on finding cheaper sources. They might, for example, put large orders out to tender. Online and web-based communications and information systems can help this process – leading to the adoption of **eprocurement**. One aspect of this might be the use of e-auctions. Ray and Ray (2006) provide an interesting example of their use by a small-to-medium business to obtain goods. The use of the web and the global nature of many businesses allow firms to exploit variations in price in different parts of the world.

E-procurement is not limited to profit-seeking organizations: for example, Birmingham City Council report having saved £1.7 million in one year by the use of e-auctions (*Computing* 3rd August 2005, page 4).

Keeping your inventory low

Large manufacturers and retailers will want to have enough stock to supply the demands of their customers. If an item is out of stock then a sale could be lost. On the other hand, having excessive stocks of finished items or components in warehouses and stockrooms is not good. Money is tied up in stock which might be better spent on other things. This is particularly a danger for fast-developing high-technology industries where businesses do not want to be left with unsold obsolete units when an upgrade of a product comes out. With technical products prices tend to fall, so stocks of components lose value. For a company like Dell 70 per cent of their costs are those of components, the buying price of which is falling by an average of 0.6 per cent a month (Magretta 1998a). Thus the ideal supplier is one which not only provides a product of good quality at a low price, but can supply it in frequent but small batches and at very short notice – this is explored further in the subsection below on 'Virtual integration'.

> **ACTIVITY 3.6 INWARD DELIVERY STRATEGY**
>
> **Consider and explain whether there is any contradiction here between the desirability of having a large number of small deliveries and the policy previously discussed of bringing small orders together to gain the discounts discussed in the subsection on 'Joint development'.**

TYPES OF SUPPLY CHAIN RELATIONSHIP

As we noted above, the supply and value chain relationships between businesses can vary in strength and quality. Below we are going to look at how the nature of the relationship can affect the technologies used to co-ordinate interactions.

One-off purchases

Here each purchase is a self-contained transaction. The supplier is just another business and no lasting relationship is established. The specification of the product is likely to be well-established and widely accepted such as, for example, the quality of paper to be used in a laser printer. As noted earlier, an eprocurement system might be used by the purchasing business to administer these orders. This would consolidate different orders for the same product in order to extract bulk discounts. As part of this approach a list of preferred suppliers might be set up – continued membership of the list might act as an incentive for suppliers to keep prices low.

Contractors

Here the product or service needed is more complex and is likely to have several components. It could be unique so that a special process would need to be carried out to create the product or service. The creation of bespoke software would be a good example of this. There would need to be a detailed discussion of the specification but once that has been agreed the actual execution of the order would be left to the judgement of the contractors. For example, they would decide on the sources for any components and on whether any activities might be sub-contracted out to other parties.

This type of relationship tends to apply to relatively self-contained projects. The relationship tends also to be '**loosely-coupled**': once the specification has been agreed information flows between the two parties will focus on project control issues and detailed operational data will not need to be passed between the parties. Extranets that hold specifications and working documents would be characteristic of the type of IT system used to support the relationship.

Network leadership

In some cases, a business can generate value by actually constructing a supply chain (Hagel III 2002). Assembly work, for example, could be profitably sub-contracted to a factory in a low-wage country. However, the managers of that factory might not be able to source the components and materials needed. Here the customer organization would have to establish the in-going supply chain into the assembly plant. Nike, known for its fashionable sportswear, does not itself actually make any of the shoes or other items that carry its logo. Instead it uses 'production partners' – the term it prefers for its suppliers – to manufacture the goods. Many of these are well-established specialist firms, but Nike also develops new resources in less developed economies such as Indonesia, China and Thailand. Nike works closely with these production partners in a 'tutelage' programme to help them develop their capabilities to supply goods to Nike's requirements. This could include working with other local businesses who supply the main local partner.

It is indicative of the variety of ways in which businesses can co-operate that the building of a customized supply chain can itself be outsourced. For instance, a fashion retailer may want to put a particular type of women's trousers into the shops to catch the time when people buy their winter clothes. The retailer could go to an organization such as the Hong Kong based Li & Fung. Li & Fung would look closely at the garment and decide on the best way to lay out the supply chain (Magretta 1998b). The yarn might come from a Korean producer, but be woven and dyed in Taiwan. The zips might come from a Japanese company that makes the zips in China. The trousers might then be made in Thailand where production could be spilt over several factories because of the need to meet the autumn deadline.

In the Li & Fung case study, the use of IT to co-ordinate operations appears relatively modest. This may be because of the shifting nature of the relationships and the lack of reliable national telecommunications in some regions. Interestingly the one IT system supporting the supply chain creation identified was used to help internal co-ordination within Li & Fung.

Virtual integration

You want to keep your holdings of components and finished units to a minimum, particularly where the value of stock tends to go down over time. Thus a business needs to co-ordinate with care its sales and the acquisition of stock.

One way of tightening control is by **vertical integration** where you bring into the organization processes that would otherwise be carried out by outsiders. This has been the traditional way that corporations have tried to control their environments. Sometimes, with fledgling technologies, companies are forced to make everything themselves as there is no-one else who could do it for them. Companies like Digital Equipment, which was once a huge presence in the computer market, had processes which created almost every part in the computers that they sold.

> Digital Equipment Corporation ceased to exist as an independent entity in 1998.

Newer entrants, such as Dell, have been able to become established in the computer market by carrying out key value creation activities in-house and sub-contracting out other activities (Magretta 1998a). This, however, leads back to the problem of control. The answer has been **virtual integration** where a relationship is built with business partners where they are treated as being inside the organization. The suppliers respond quickly to many frequent small orders for the delivery of components which are delivered quickly. This is enabled by having shared information systems that allow a close synchronization of the operations of the two organizations.

The second part of the solution is that Dell have effective methods of assessing the demand for their products. In part this is helped by having a large number of institutions and corporations as customers. By building close relationships with these customers, insights can be gained about future plans for the purchase of IT equipment.

TECHNOLOGY ISSUES

Virtual integration clearly needs IT support in the form of shared information systems. This is an area fraught with difficulties. Most substantial enterprises will have **enterprise resource planning (ERP)** applications. ERP systems integrate generic IS applications that were formerly separate.

Each component application that carries out the processing of business transactions such as purchasing, order tracking, inventory maintenance and sales is a 'module' and the system owner can choose which modules to acquire from the ERP system supplier.

> ERP is discussed in more detail in Chapter 5.

Virtual integration often means that the ERP systems of two or more enterprises have to be integrated to some extent and the relatively self-contained OTS nature of these applications can cause a barrier. However, as will be seen in Chapter 5, the problem can be alleviated if the same ERP system is being used by both parties and the ERP vendor has facilitated links.

One approach is for the dominant partner (or **network leader**) to create an **extranet** – essentially an intranet made accessible to their suppliers. These extranet users can access data and even input transactions to the other organization's information system. However, this system is not the supplier's: each customer that they supply could have their own system. Input to these systems is therefore likely to involve manual re-keying of data which is time-consuming and prone to error.

> Innocent, which produces fruit juices, uses EDI to communicate with its customer, Asda, and has an extranet to communicate with its suppliers (*Computing* 19 January 2006, p. 30).

An alternative approach which gets around these problems is for an independent intermediary, usually dedicated to the industrial sector, to be established which acts as an 'electronic market place' for the industry. At one time the technology for such exchanges was based on EDI which predates the web and can operate separately to it. An example of such a system was CitiusNet. The pervasiveness of the web now favours web-based platforms.

A key question is whether it is worthwhile for a supplier to develop an automated link with a major customer. This would involve investment by the supplier and so they would need to be convinced that the benefits would justify the expense. Some have argued that advances in software technologies, such as **service-oriented architecture**, will eventually reduce the cost of setting up such links. The main web protocol, HTTP, assumes that at the client end there is a human being with a browser. SOAP allows software programs running under different operating systems to send each other messages using the HTTP protocol and without a human mediator. SOAP uses XML to put the data to be transferred into a format the receiving system will be able to decode. It is argued that the existing applications at each end of the transfer can remain unchanged so that this technical solution should be relatively straightforward to implement.

> Service-oriented architecture is an extension of the idea of web services introduced in Chapter 1.

For such a solution to be possible, common formats for the most frequent types of communication in an industrial sector have to be agreed. Once agreed, these formats are encoded using XML. In the automotive industries, for example, there is the ANX standard while the chemical industry has CIDX.

To balance the costs of developing such links there must be benefits and for smaller suppliers these benefits may not be obvious. It is always easy for outsiders to over-estimate the sophistication of the technologies actually in use in industry. A survey (Buxman et al. 2004) of the actual use of supply chain management software in the European car industry found that almost 66 per cent of respondents did not use IT applications for supply chain management. However, 14 per cent of respondents, who would also be counted within the 66 per cent above, were in the process of implementing such systems. The most common reason given for not using such software was that enough benefit from using it had not been found.

CONCLUSION

Some technological advances enable enterprises to invest in innovations that let them carry out their existing business activities more effectively. This might be the case where processes can be automated and staff savings can be made. These are **sustaining innovations**.

Other innovations can threaten an enterprise by destroying its existing business. This could be the case when someone creates a new product that is a substitute for one produced by the enterprise. These **disruptive innovations** are much more difficult to deal with.

The development of the web has been a sustaining innovation for some industries and a disruptive one for others. A key lesson is the need for a business to scan carefully and continually the environment in which it operates and the next chapter explores this lesson further.

SELF-TEST QUESTIONS

1. In the Porter value chain model, to which of the generic value creating activities does the delivery of finished products to customers belong?

   (a) Operations.
   (b) Outward logistics.
   (c) Marketing and sales.
   (d) Services.

2. A firm of solicitors would be most likely to conform to which of the following value models?

   (a) Value chain.
   (b) Value shop.
   (c) Value network.
   (d) Value tree.

3. Rather than buying insurance from an insurance broker, you buy it directly from the insurance company. This is an example of which of the following?

   (a) Disintermediation.
   (b) Disaggregation.
   (c) Virtual integration.
   (d) Vertical integration.

4. A business sells clothes via a website and generates good profits. It decides to re-invest some of these profits to buy its main supplier. Of which of the following is this an example?

   (a) Re-intermediation.
   (b) Cannibalization.
   (c) Channel conflict.
   (d) Vertical integration.

5. Which of the following is LEAST true?

   (a) Stock levels should be kept low as it reduces the need for working capital.
   (b) Stock should be kept at a level that ensures there is enough stock to meet customers' orders.
   (c) High stock levels may mean that money may be lost if a product is replaced by a newer more attractive product.
   (d) Having large amounts of stock is like having money in the bank – the more the better.

4 The Business and Technological Environment

LEARNING OUTCOMES

When you have completed this chapter you should be able to demonstrate an understanding of the following:

- the use of SWOT analysis to help you think about the opportunities a business may be able to exploit and the threats with which it must cope;
- how political, economic and social developments need to be taken into account when assessing a proposal for an ebusiness development;
- the nature of technological change, in particular the factors influencing the acceptance of an innovation;
- the assessment of the business opportunities offered by a particular technological innovation;
- the need to be sensitive to the interplay between ethical, legal and political issues that might affect an ebusiness development.

INTRODUCTION

In Chapter 2 we looked at the competitive strength of an individual business when dealing with its suppliers and customers and also in Chapter 3 its situation in the broader network of organizations that make up a supply chain. We considered the effects of information technologies (ITs) on these relationships. The use of the internet was seen to favour buyers at the expense of sellers because buyers are able to find the lowest prices more easily. With the supply chain, ITs could enable more precise co-ordination between businesses and their suppliers. This allows them to cut the costs of having large buffer stocks.

Historically there has been a tendency for IT business analysts to concentrate on the internal processes of an organization and to seek ways of making them more efficient. Usually this was driven by a desire to reduce staff costs. Technologies were adopted to support streamlined work methods: for example, using shared corporate databases to remove duplicated data records. However, previously we stressed the need to look beyond simple efficiency gains and to pay attention to the generation of value.

Also, IT-focused business development has tended to be motivated by a need to solve a particular problem – a mismatch between what currently exists and what should, but does not. A problem is thus a circumstance which causes people difficulties of which they are only too aware. However, new technologies can create new opportunities – improving existing conditions and generating value in areas where no-one has previously considered there to be problems. The use of texting on a mobile phone is a modest example of this. Clearly texting can be a very useful feature. Yet as a substitute for voice communication it is not something that many people would have originally identified as a key requirement for mobile phone users. The prevalence for texting has to a large extent come spontaneously from grass-roots consumers, but has subsequently been exploited by large-scale IS developers as a means of sending individuals time-critical and personal information, such as notification of important events.

The conventional wisdom in information systems has been that the use of technology should be driven by information processing requirements which in turn should be driven by business need. There have clearly been examples where this principle has not been followed and computerization seemed to be pursued for its own sake and on shaky financial grounds. However, there is a justification for looking at new technologies to see what opportunities they present without necessarily a specific need in mind. There may be applications that no-one has previously considered. Thomas Edison invented the original phonograph for the dictation of office memos – the idea of recording music only emerged later (Naughton 1999, p. 248). Tim Berners-Lee originally saw the web as a means of managing documentation and is claimed to have been shocked by the development of a multimedia browser. Thus more recently there has been much examination of the uses to which RFID tags can be put and some of these possible applications might not have been immediately obvious – such as the tagging of surgery patients in hospitals. This evaluation is ongoing as reductions in the cost of the technology increase the range of possible applications.

The upshot of all this is that an exclusive focus on the current internal state of a business is not enough. The environment in which a business lives needs to be scanned periodically for new developments. These are not just advances in technology, but can also relate to changes in economic, social and political conditions. Such developments can offer opportunities, but as we have seen in the last chapter they can also be disruptive changes that can threaten the viability of a business.

SWOT ANALYSIS

SWOT analysis is a framework to help you think about the **strengths** and **weaknesses** of a business. The analysis also helps you to look out for **opportunities** that the strengths of the business may allow it to exploit.

It also allows you to identify the **threats** to the business that could play upon the weaknesses.

> SWOT stands for **S**trengths, **W**eaknesses, **O**pportunities and **T**hreats.

Opportunities and threats generally relate to the future and will almost always emerge from the wider environment in which a business operates.

In a competitive world, a key consideration is how you compare with your competitors. One weakness that you might identify, for example, might be a high turnover of technically skilled staff. If all your competitors also suffer from the same problem, this might suggest that there is something in the current labour market that affects everyone. You might not therefore worry unduly about this, but if there was some way of addressing the problem inexpensively this could give you an advantage over your competitors. Thus a SWOT analysis of a business, to be effective, needs to be accompanied by SWOT analyses of its competitors.

> ### ACTIVITY 4.1 SWOT ANALYSIS
>
> **Spend a few minutes comparing the strengths, weaknesses, opportunities and threats that affect the use of mobile phones and PC-based email.**

When SWOT is applied to a business it should help identify problems that need to be solved and opportunities that need to be exploited. It should lead to recommendations about future courses of action.

SWOT analysis could also be applied to a proposed change. The analysis might look at the strengths, weaknesses, opportunities and threats that would exist once a proposal had been implemented.

ENVIRONMENTAL SCANNING

Environmental scanning describes the process of seeking out possible threats and opportunities to a business in its environment.

Mnemonics have been devised to provide checklists of the types of factors that should be considered. **STEP analysis** originally covered:

- **Sociocultural** factors;
- **Technical** factors;
- **Economic** factors;
- **Political** factors.

Some have used the mnemonic **PEST**. Others have added **legal** and **environmental** factors which gives us either **PESTLE** or **PESTEL**. Environmental issues – relating to things such as carbon emissions – are clearly becoming more pressing. **Ethical** issues have also been suggested as needing consideration. In this chapter we have responded to this by considering environmental issues to be a particular type of ethical issue.

It is tempting to suggest that the mnemonic should now be STEEPLE.

Use of these checklists can help ensure that important areas in the environment are not missed. It will be seen that many developments straddle more than one category, particularly between social and economic changes and between political and legal ones. As long as the important issues are identified their categorization does not matter too much.

ACTIVITY 4.2 A LIFTS DATABASE: ENVIRONMENTAL SCANNING

A proposal is being put forward for a web-based car-sharing application. People willing to give lifts to others on either a one-off or regular basis will be able to find passengers and vice versa. Using the seven environmental categories identified above, draw up a list of bullet points of issues that would need to be investigated.

The framework is a way of prompting questions and initiating enquires. Not all factors will have a bearing on all development proposals. For some proposals there might, for example, be no political ramifications. However, the checklist just makes us pause for thought and think about possible problems. In the lifts database example in Activity 4.2, for instance, it would prompt us to consider legal implications. This might raise questions about the legal position if it was agreed that the driver and passengers should share fuel costs. Would this mean the car was legally being used for hire, and could this affect the driver's insurance cover and tax position? The drafters of the proposal would need to go away and do some homework.

In fact, if the driver is not making a profit from the activity, the insurance and tax positions should not be affected (Department for Transport 2004).

Below we are going to explore some of the issues that can emerge from constituent parts of environment scanning. There is no claim that this is by any means an exhaustive survey. We are going to start with social factors and then go on to technological factors as there is considerable interplay between these two.

SOCIOCULTURAL FACTORS

Among the things that could be considered under this heading are (Johnson and Scholes 2002):

- demography;
- income distribution;
- social mobility;
- lifestyle changes;
- attitudes to work and leisure;
- consumerism;
- education.

ACTIVITY 4.3 ENABLERS AND BARRIERS TO GLOBAL REACH

"There has never been a commercial technology like this in the history of the world, whereby the minute you adopt it, it forces you to think and act globally."

Robert Hormats, Deputy Chairman of Goldman Sachs International, quoted in Cairncross (2001, p. 95)

Identify the reasons why the use of the internet and web might force organizations to think globally. Does this mean that all ebusinesses must be global? Are there barriers to global reach?

As we can see from Activity 4.3, because of the potential global reach of the internet we need to think more carefully about who our customers are likely to be. If they are going to come from other countries and cultures we need to make sure we are not making unwarranted assumptions.

Someone with an ebusiness proposal, particularly if it is a consumer-oriented B2C application, needs to assess the number of potential customers. In Chapter 2 we discussed the idea of **market segments** – that different groups of customers have different characteristics and different reasons for wanting your product or service. Designers of computer interfaces often devise **personas**, imagined individuals who are seen as typical of those expected to use the interface. While we are not completely convinced about the use of personas – real users must be better than imagined ones – there is a need to have a clear idea of the kind of people who will be the customer. **Demography** can be the starting point. The United Nations have defined demography as 'the scientific study of human populations, primarily with respect to their size, their structure and their development'. A very obvious example of the importance of demography would be if you decided to sell a novel form of baby-buggy. Here customers would be new or prospective parents. The baby-buggy innovator would need to study statistics relating to projected birth rates and the disposable income of typical new parents in order to start to get an idea of the maximum size of the market and of an attractive price.

Where a proposed application is B2C, then a key question would be the proportion of the target market that uses the internet.

Where a proposal for an ebusiness application intends to exploit the global reach of the internet, then potential regional and cultural differences need to be investigated. Where a website is selling fashionable clothing or cosmetics, for example, raunchy images may be less acceptable in some cultures than others. Local differences can be quite subtle: for example, in Europe some countries have been less willing to use credit cards than others – there may be a practice of paying on delivery (Cairncross 2001, p. 108).

Cultural differences can create effective barriers to cross-border trade. A major barrier could of course be language. To reach 70 per cent of Europeans requires the use of five languages. It is true that English (or perhaps more accurately American) has tended to become a global means of communication. However, some countries in Europe are much more willing to use English as a second language than others. On the other hand, because English is the second language for so many people, it means that non-native English speakers with different first languages can use English to communicate. Britons need to be aware that international English is not the same as British English – it is a simplified subset. Thus colloquialisms – often unintended – need to be avoided in text on websites aimed at an international market.

> **Localization** refers to the customization (including translation) of a software product for a local, usually national, market.

TECHNOLOGICAL FACTORS

We have already, in Chapter 2, touched on the problem that if a new business idea is really successful, then it will not be long before other entrepreneurs will be looking for ways of copying the idea. Thus an easily copied idea will not be **sustainable** in the long term. One twist to this is that many innovations need **complementary technologies** or assets – thus iPods need iTunes in order to download music. One danger is that an innovator may find that they themselves do not benefit as much as the owner of the complementary technology. For example, the first spreadsheet Visicalc that was created by Dan Bricklin and Bob Frankston was soon copied by others but it encouraged many people to buy the early microcomputers. This benefited the makers of microcomputers, particularly the Apple II.

The diffusion of innovation

Even when an innovation has a clear advantage over the previous way of doing things the public will not flock to the innovation in one large crowd.

Everett Rogers (1983) has spent a lifetime studying the way that new ideas are adopted – or abandoned – by populations. Rogers noted that when an innovation does sweep through society – the use of the internet is a prime example here – the accumulative uptake starts off very slowly as it takes time for people to learn about the new idea and decide they want to try it out. If the innovation takes hold then the number of adopters will gradually increase to a peak, and then adoption will start to slow down as the last adopters, perhaps very reluctantly, come on board. If this is drawn as a curve on a graph then the classic bell-shape emerges – see Figure 4.1.

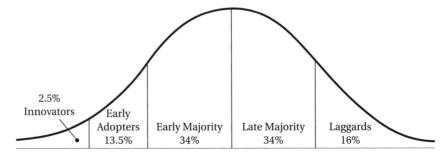

FIGURE 4.1   *Roger's diffusion of innovation curve (from Rogers (1983))*

Rogers also observed that the people who took up the new idea at different stages in the cycle in Figure 4.1 had different characteristics which he defined as follows.

- **Innovators (2.5%).** Rogers labelled these as 'venturesome'. The first people to try something out are probably driven to a large extent by innate curiosity.
- **Early adopters (13.5%).** These were labelled as 'respectable'. They were perhaps among the first 'serious' users who are not using the innovation simply for the sake of it.
- **Early majority (34%).** Rogers called these 'deliberate' users, suggesting that the benefits of using innovation have now been well-established.
- **Late majority (34%).** These are people who have been 'sceptical' but have rather reluctantly been won over.
- **Laggards (16%).** These are the traditionalists who have really dragged their feet.

Most innovations have two important elements. One is the product itself, the other is knowledge about how to use the product effectively. It is not much use buying an expensive car, even if you can well afford it, if you cannot drive it. The adoption of innovation is closely related to a knowledge diffusion process concerned with its mode of use.

> Rogers referred to 'software' as an analogy for the knowledge element – but this is confusing as there is often a software component embedded in the product itself.

Early adopters tend to be among the better educated. Being some of the first to get to grips with the new idea means that there are lot of things to find out that later adopters can take for granted. In order to be an early adopter you need to hear about the innovation – early adopters tend to have wider contacts than other people, interacting with a range of sources of information.

A major paradox is that although we are more likely to learn more from people who are different from ourselves, we are more likely to trust people who we feel are the same as us. In order for an innovation to take hold people who are **opinion leaders** need to be seen to be adopting and supporting the innovation. A key characteristic of opinion leaders is that they tend to be people with whom we can identify. When we want a recommendation or advice about a new technology we usually prefer to talk to someone who speaks in a way we can understand. The opinion leader is therefore unlikely to be someone who is a 'geek' – unless we are geeks too.

The idea of **viral marketing** can be seen as an attempt to exploit the way in which the adoption of an innovation spreads. Here marketers target people they think are opinion leaders and perhaps provide them with a free sample of the product. The hope is that they will take it up in a big way and their followers will emulate them.

Adoption of a new product or service is not inevitable. Certain characteristics seem to favour the success of new ideas and products.

- **Relative advantage.** If the new product or service does not have obvious advantages over the existing state of affairs then potential customers will see little point in taking it up.
- **Compatibility.** This favours new products and services that can be adopted without the consumer having to make huge changes. If, for example, a new, potentially useful, software product can be executed on your existing hardware and operating system platforms and can work with existing software then it is more likely to be adopted.
- **Complexity.** If a new product is difficult to understand and use then this will be a barrier to acceptance.
- **Trialability.** Is it possible to put a toe in the water or is it a question of all or nothing? Where a leap of faith is needed then adopters will be naturally cautious.
- **Observability.** If the benefits of the innovation are quickly and concretely experienced and outsiders can see the benefits, then the innovation is more likely to be taken up.

ACTIVITY 4.4 ASSESSING BARRIERS TO ADOPTION

Assess the relative ease of adoption of the following innovations.

(a) Eprocurement in a local authority.

(Continued)

(Continued)

(b) **'Self-service' online updating of personnel details such as names and addresses and bank details on a human resources administration system by staff working in a supermarket.**

(c) **Replacement of a sales ordering application, developed in-house, by a customized off-the-shelf (COTS) application supplied by an external specialist software supplier.**

Innovation and the network effect

In addition to the product specific characteristics that might encourage or discourage adoption, there are other more general factors that could affect adoption (Fichman and Kemmerer 1993). These would be more relevant where there is a **network effect**, that is, the success of an innovation depends on not just you adopting the technology, but others too. The internet and mobile phones are good examples of this.

- **Prior technology drag.** There is an investment, financial and otherwise, in an existing technology that the innovation will make obsolete. This will discourage adoption of the innovation. An organization might be in a business where there are a large number of complex business rules embedded in their legacy software. This software may be written in a programming language that is now out of vogue. If the move to a new more productive software environment was proposed, then the question of re-writing the old core software would have to be considered. Often the final decision is to retain and maintain the legacy software. This is because re-writing the existing functionality rather than fulfilling new requirements may not be attractive. **Upwards compatibility** is often a design requirement with new products – for example, that a new version of a word-processing application should still be able to read documents created by previous versions.

- **Irreversibility of investments.** If the adoption of an innovation will involve investing in changes which will be difficult or impossible to reverse then this may discourage adoption. Thus, for example, an organization needs to think carefully about its outsourcing arrangements, as outsourcing could effectively destroy an in-house capability, thus removing the option to bring that operation back in-house at a later date.

- **Sponsorship.** If there is a powerful body that defines technological and other standards and actively promotes the innovation then this can encourage adoption. The sponsor may be in a powerful position where it can mandate the use of a standard in a significant part of the user community. This is the case with the UK government which mandates the use of the PRINCE2 project management standard in public sector projects. Recently there has been a contest between two new competing High Density video disk technologies, each sponsored by a consortium of industry organizations with a financial interest in the developments.

• **Expectations.** If there is a widespread conviction that there will eventually be universal adoption of the new standard, this will encourage its acceptance. It is often the case that those with a vested interest in adoption of a standard will use sponsoring bodies to orchestrate the impression that the progress of a certain technology is inevitable.

A major risk with the adoption of innovations that benefit from network effects is that of **stranding**: a prospective standard is picked which in fact does not become widely accepted and an organization is left with a technology that is not compatible with much of the rest of the world with which it interacts. Even when a new standard does take off, being one of the first adopters may be more expensive than waiting for a while before moving over. There will be extra costs, not just as you learn by your mistakes, but in overcoming the problems of interacting with people who have not yet adopted the technology. These are called **transient compatibility costs**.

> What can be particularly annoying is that the stranded technology can sometimes be technically superior to the successful one.

User perceptions of a technology

It was argued earlier that it was worth examining new technologies to see if they could create opportunities which could be exploited. We will look at one of the ways in which this can be done.

We often talk about 'applications' as in 'IT applications' or 'software applications'. We mean the application of a particular technology to carry out a required task. In each case we need to judge whether the technology would be effective.

The answer will depend on the ease with which potential users can apply the technology to carry out the task. Some users will use an application because they have no choice. It may be that they are sales orders clerks and the only way that they are going to take an order that someone has phoned in is by input to a computer. For other applications – such as computer games – use is entirely voluntary. Importantly for ebusiness, the consumers who use a website to purchase goods will be doing so largely of their own free will.

ACTIVITY 4.5 MEASURING ATTRACTIVENESS

The ISO 9126 international standard (ISO/IEE 2001, 2003) has a new software quality called 'attractiveness'. Existing software qualities have measurements associated with them, for example mean time between failures for the quality of reliability. Can attractiveness be objectively measured? If so, how?

The difference between mandatory and voluntary use is not a clear-cut, binary one. In a commercial context, for example, the use of email might notionally be optional but you could be under strong pressure to use it if you wished to remain in business.

With voluntary users there are two major elements that encourage use. One is the **perceived usefulness** (PU) of the application. If you feel that you have nothing to gain from using the application – this could include at least some amusement – then you are not going to waste time learning how to use it. Once you decide to use it, then the next hurdle is the **perceived ease of use** (PEU). If the application is difficult to use at some point you may decide you have had enough and give up. This point is likely to vary depending on how great the PU is: if using a particular B2C site is the only way you can buy something you really want at a price much cheaper than elsewhere, then you are likely to persevere despite poor navigation. The fact that potential users will not automatically use an online service if it is offered to them is illustrated by a report by Forrester Research (Ensor 2006) that while about a half of European investors use the internet on a regular basis only a quarter of them access their investment accounts online.

> This description is based on the **Technology Acceptance Model** – see Davis (1989).

Some of the barriers to use will be because of poor implementation of the technology, for instance poor interface design. In other cases it will be because of limitations in the technology itself. A new technology will have both advantages and constraints, and good application design and implementation may involve finding ways of getting around these constraints.

Evaluating a new technology

Once someone has started to use the application then there is still the question of whether it carries out the required task effectively. This can be judged by assessing the **task-technology fit** (TTF), the degree to which the technology is good at supporting a particular type of task (Goodhue and Thompson 1995). You would often have a particular application of the technology in mind, for instance using RFID to identify goods in a warehouse. However, as we noted in the introduction to this chapter, it may be possible to analyse a technology and identify the generic situations where it could be effective. For example, Judith Gebauer, Michael J. Shaw and Kexin Zhao (Gebauer et al. 2002) found the following opportunities and constraints offered by the use of mobile phones to access information systems.

Opportunities

- Wider reach – access is not confined to an office or desk.
- There is faster access to applications.
- The possibility of integrating voice and data input exists.
- Some people are more familiar with mobile phones than PCs.
- The device is relatively simple to use.
- Mass production means they are cheap to buy.

Constraints

- Small display.
- Small number of keys.
- Limited ability to input data.
- Uneven signal availability.
- Lack of security.
- Expensive per minute charges when compared to PC internet access.

From this a number of **windows of opportunity** to gain value from mobile phone interfaces were identified where the following situations existed:

- A task is urgent and is triggered by someone requesting permission from a manager to do something.
- A task is a simple update: it does not require the mobile phone user to navigate through a complicated menu structure or to access multiple databases.
- The transaction requires voice and data communication.
- Data security is not an issue.
- A member of staff may sometimes need to respond urgently to a request to carry out a task.
- The person required to carry out the task is often working outside an office environment.

The list of windows of opportunity can be used to pinpoint places where the use of mobile phone technology could be usefully adopted. For example, this might be to notify a van driver on the road that a consignment due for delivery is now ready for collection.

Where there is only a partial match then steps might be considered to bridge the gap between the requirement and the technology. Say that it is suggested that an onsite technician should have the facility to provide an immediate price quotation for new work required by the customer. It may be that a normal mobile telephone handset would be inadequate and a more substantial device would need to be considered.

Technologies are usually in a continuing process of development and so checklists like the one above would need to be regularly reviewed and updated as constraints are overcome.

ACTIVITY 4.6 POTENTIAL USES OF MOBILE PHONES AS AN INPUT DEVICE

Consider the feasibility of the possible application of mobile phones as an input and display device for the following tasks:

(a) Using a mobile phone to instruct your bank to make a payment to a third party.

(b) Renewing a monthly railway season ticket.

(c) Being notified automatically of traffic problems when driving on a motorway.

(d) Notifying a software engineer of a problem requiring attention and providing a means for the engineer to type instructions to remedy a fault if one has been found.

ACTIVITY 4.7 POTENTIAL USES OF RFID AND GPS

Outline some of the key generic features of the situations where RFID could be useful. How could a global positioning system (GPS) be able to add value beyond that offered by RFID in the situations that you have identified?

ECONOMIC FACTORS

Any proposal for ebusiness development should take account of the current economic climate and probable future trends. Among the economic variables that should be considered are the following factors.

- **Business cycles.** Economies tend to have cycles: over time there is a succession of periods of more and less favourable economic conditions. While there are massive interdependencies between many national economies, there can still be local variations. One consequence of this is that exchange rates between currencies can vary. A strong pound against the US dollar will make it cheaper to buy goods in the US but make UK exports to that country more expensive.

- **Interest rates.** If interest rates are high potential consumers may have less money to spend on new products if they have higher debt repayments on house mortgages. If the acquisition of an innovative product or service requires considerable financial outlay, then restrictions on credit may discourage some purchases. On the other side, entrepreneurs who need to borrow money to finance their business proposals will find loans more expensive.

- **Inflation** is the general propensity for prices to rise over time. Price rises are not inevitable – the products of new technologies tend in fact to decrease in price over time as manufacturers learn to become more efficient, and the initial development and set-up costs are gradually paid off. Some businesses are particularly dependent on raw materials or other inputs such as electricity. Possible price rises in these purchases will need to be taken into account. Electricity consumption has been highlighted as a concern for large data centres (Watson 2006). Developments in technology mean that more servers can be packed into racks, leading to a greater concentration of these devices and greater demands for power. It is said that a 30,000 square foot server farm can consume the same amount of power as 2,000 to 2,500 homes. On one site it has been calculated that the cost of electricity over three years will exceed the cost of acquiring the servers. It has also been reported that one facility in Manchester had room to expand, but not enough power.

    The 'headline' inflation rates are calculated using the prices of a selection of goods and services. Different sections of the public will in fact suffer or benefit in different ways from changes in prices depending on the kind of things that they spend their money on.
- **Unemployment.** If unemployment rises then the disposable income of those laid off will fall. Higher unemployment tends to be associated with lower wage levels and vice versa.

The factors listed above are more general macroeconomic ones. There will also be more specific detailed economic decisions about things such as the pricing structure to be adopted for a particular product.

All the components of PESTLE analysis are inter-related. It can sometimes be difficult to decide whether a local difference is in fact essentially socially or economically driven. For example, historically the US has been less enthusiastic about the use of mobile phones than Europe and elsewhere. Elaborate explanations based on the differences in culture can be suggested. However, in this case it can be convincingly argued that the reluctance to use mobile phones is economically based. In the US a 'called-party-pays' system where you are charged for receiving mobile phone calls has deterred the use of mobile phones (Cairncross 2001, p. 56).

The term pricing structure refers not just to the actual price but the way that the price is calculated for an individual. With internet services, such as broadband, there is often a question of whether to adopt 'pay-as-you-go' or a fixed amount regardless of usage. There is some evidence that where customers know that they will make good use of a service, they prefer to pay a fixed price rather than pay by use – even if their actual usage often makes it a more expensive option (Odlyzko 2001).

Finally, it should be noted that the circumstances, economic or otherwise, that cause difficulties for the many can also generate pockets of opportunity. The security measures introduced at British airports in the summer of 2006 led to airports and airlines losing large amounts of money because of cancelled flights – the British Airports Authority, for example, lost £13 million (Milmo 2006). However, Frankie & Benny's and Chiquito restaurants reported that the crisis had contributed to their profits as waiting passengers had spent more money at their airport outlets (Barriaux 2006).

ETHICAL, LEGAL AND POLITICAL FACTORS

The interplay between ethics, law and politics

The remaining three factors that we will consider concerning ethics, the law and politics are all closely related. Ethical behaviour is that which is regarded as morally correct: even though a course of action is legal it does not mean that it will be regarded as morally acceptable. As various religious and moral controversies illustrate, there is often a lack of universal agreement about what is in fact morally acceptable. Despite this there is usually a considerable consensus about what constitutes individual anti-social behaviour: behaviour that harms other people in the community, especially those who are vulnerable such as young children.

Where it is felt that some behaviour is technically legal but is morally repugnant or socially damaging then this may lead to a political campaign to create laws to physically suppress that behaviour. An example in the US is the successful political campaign to ban online gambling (Clark 2006).

In the context of ebusiness ethical issues have come to the fore because the internet has created a vast new space for human interaction which has very little regulation. It can be seen as a kind of Wild West frontier where lawlessness can reign (Newton 2004, p. 112). The global nature of this space means that there is no single legal jurisdiction to monitor and control all activity on the internet. The novelty of the internet also means that some safeguards that most people would expect to enjoy have to be specifically extended to the new medium. Thus, the Computer Misuse Act 1990 was brought in to outlaw deliberate malicious damage through hacking.

The need for trust

There is a huge literature on ethics, including its application to business practice. The one point that we wish to explore here is that apart from anything else unethical behaviour in the business world has some very practical consequences. If there are perceptions of lawlessness in the world of the internet then people will be reluctant to use it to do business. Practices that seem unfair and personally damaging lead to distrust and a disinclination to buy and sell.

On an individual business level successful B2C sites have tended to be the ones that have a very liberal **returns policy** so that the purchasers' anxieties that items bought unseen might not meet their expectations have been reduced. This has promoted trust and has been a significant contributor to the growth of customer loyalty.

Factors contributing to customer trust include **ease of communication** with the company (Schneider 2003, p. 131, Schulze and Baumgartner 2001, p. 33). There is evidence that where a customer has a problem which is dealt with effectively by a supplier, the customer is more likely to be satisfied with the business than where there has been no problem at all (Stalhane et al. 1997). In the light of this, it will be interesting to see the actions taken by easyJet.com who have been the subject of numerous complaints by customers trying to communicate with the company when, for example, trying to seek refunds for flights they had cancelled (Brignall 2006a).

> easyJet is only one example. A survey by Netcall (Collinson 2006) found that phone queues of 30 minutes were very common generally. An ethical issue is that, in the UK, 0870 and 0871 numbers mean that the customer pays for these calls.

A special problem with trust is C2C ebusinesses such as eBay and Amazon when dealing with used goods. A centralizing hub brings together individual buyers and sellers. Here the hub cannot inspect the goods for sale. A system whereby purchasers can rate and publish their evaluation of the service provided by a seller is used to foster confidence in carrying out purchases.

The concern about customer trust is exemplified by eBay's launch of eBay Express which sells new goods from established brands that have been vetted by eBay. A returns policy and guaranteed delivery date are publicized. This, it is hoped, will attract more cautious customers who are wary of the core eBay facility (Allen 2006).

A new ebusiness activity can also enhance trust by obtaining **sponsorship** or **endorsement** by an existing trusted organization. There are also assurance providers such as TrustE which inspect websites and ebusiness procedures and will certify that they will conform to codes of practice for privacy and security. The organization also undertakes to investigate complaints made by users of certified websites.

Because all trade depends to such a large degree on trust, businesses will collaborate to create frameworks to promote trust through such things as electronic marketplaces that are regulated by the businesses that use them. Trade organizations are established that attempt to **accredit** the competence of practitioners, to set **standards** for work practices and products, and to provide **arbitration** services for dissatisfied customers. Because commerce is so important to the economic well-being of communities governments will sometimes feel obliged to intervene to impose legislation.

European Union regulation

The European Community has been active in this area as an important part of its mission is the establishment of a Europe-wide free trade area. One element of this has been encouraging people in different European Community countries to buy from and sell to each other via the internet. To this end, European Union (EU) directives have been promulgated to encourage ecommerce. An EU directive is an instruction to each member state to introduce local laws to enforce an agreed community policy. Directives set out the required outcome – it leaves the precise way of achieving that outcome in law to each member state. Some of the more relevant directives for ebusiness have been the Electronic Commerce Directive, the Distance Selling Directive, the Electronic Signatures Directive and the Directive on Electronic Money Institutions.

> A good general introduction to the law as it applies to IT is Holt and Newton (2004).

One outcome of this is that there are legal requirements relating to the disclosure of information with which an ebusiness website must comply if it is buying or selling goods or services. The information to be displayed includes:

* **name and geographic address** of the trader;
* **contact details;**
* **trade register details** – details of any trade or equivalent register in which the trader is listed;
* **relevant professional membership** – details of any professional body with which the trader is registered, including a registration number so that membership can be verified and details of how the code of conduct for the professional body can be accessed;
* **VAT registration number.**

Traders are also required to provide precise details of the goods or services to be supplied – including details of any possible substitutions – and the conditions of sale. The customer must be allowed to cancel an order that has been placed within a specified time limit, normally 30 days. There are some exceptions to this. The details of the sale must be confirmed via an independent and permanent medium – this can be email as the customers can make a paper copy of the email.

Other legal requirements

Other areas where the legal implications of an ebusiness proposal must be investigated include:

- advertising standards;
- defamation and libel;
- copyright and other intellectual property rights;
- data protection and privacy;
- taxation on ecommerce;
- domain names and trademarks.

> An example of a dispute over trademarks is an action in 2006 by Apple Corps, the record company formed by The Beatles, and Apple Computer in relation to the operation of iTunes.

For example each of the following could infringe someone's intellectual property rights:

- copying the complete layout of a website;
- using data obtained from a database that is part of another website;
- linking to pages from another website, but not making clear that they are not yours.

Data protection legislation requires websites to inform users about cookies and covert software that might be collecting information about them. Data subjects must be able to correct mistaken information that is held about them. Unsolicited emails must not be sent to customers who have not given their permission.

The strategic implications of intellectual property

In Chapter 2 we saw that a novel idea for a new product or an improved process could give the innovator a competitive advantage over other entrepreneurs in the same market. However, the innovator might not benefit from this for long if the new product or way of doing things was copied by competitors.

One way of prolonging the lead over competitors is through **patents** (Jolly 2006a). Patents are very powerful as they give the patent-holder a legally enforceable monopoly. In the case of copyright infringement it must be shown that the infringer actually had access to the original article and made a copy of it. Copyright does not give you any rights where a technologist independently arrives at a similar outcome to yours. Unlike copyright, it is possible to contravene a patent even though you are unaware that it exists.

Patenting products and processes can be central to the strategy of a business. In the UK and the rest of Europe, patents must be technical in nature, but the US allows a broader range of things to be patented. Large corporations therefore often take out patents as a pre-emptive measure. Software, it should be noted, is classified in the UK for the purposes of intellectual property law as 'literature' and is therefore subject to copyright rather than patent law, unless the patent relates to a hardware system which has software to control it.

Successful patents allow innovators to build and sell the product themselves, or to generate income by granting licences to use the technology to others. The latter course of action might be followed if the innovator did not have the resources to exploit fully the new idea.

> The chip innovator ARM has adopted a strategy based on granting others licences to use its technology (Jolly 2006b).

Political intervention to promote competition

In previous chapters, emphasis has been placed on the competitiveness of the business world. The Porter five forces model discussed in Chapter 2 also drew attention to the influences on the relative power of buyers and sellers. Where a business entity grows to dominate a particular market – Microsoft quickly comes to mind – then it can gain huge power. When you 'buy' an item of software from Microsoft you enter a contractual relationship with them which gives you permission to use the software. As an individual you are hardly in a position to negotiate with a large corporation like Microsoft, so governments tend to introduce legislation – an example of which is the 30-day cancellation period for distance selling transactions mentioned above – to give specific protection to consumers.

Large monopolies can exert huge influence that can work against the general effect of competition to reduce prices. Governments will therefore intervene to break existing monopolies, as in the case of national telecommunications companies in Europe, where, for example, the monopoly position of British Telecom in the UK was removed in 1984. Governments may intervene where it appears that a business has acquired a prominent position and appears to abuse that position by unfairly stifling competitors. For example, the EU Competition Commission controversially forced Microsoft to produce a version of the Windows operating environment that did not have the Windows Media Player and fined Microsoft €497 million on the grounds that providing the 'free' media player was unfair to other suppliers of media players (Gow 2006). Governments can also intervene where businesses in the same market reduce price competition by agreeing to fix prices.

Other compliance demands

In the wake of Enron and other corporate scandals, governments have become increasingly concerned about making the dealings of businesses more transparent. The argument is that where a corporation is compelled to record fully and permanently the details of each transaction it carries out, then the chances of undetected illegal activities are reduced.

The Sarbanes–Oxley Act of 2002 in the US – known variously as 'Sarbox' or 'Sox' for short – requires that companies keep accurate records which are archived and can be readily retrieved. To remove the scope for bureaucratic buck-passing chief executives are held personally responsible for signing off annual figures (Williams 2006). These requirements apply to companies registered in the US, but given the considerable number of US organizations operating in Europe, they have had a considerable impact on IT development in this country. Some London-based gaming companies have sought to circumvent US state laws against online gambling by basing themselves outside US jurisdiction. The response has been that the US Congress has passed a law making it illegal for banks in the US to process electronic payments for these offshore gambling websites (Wray 2006a,b).

> As we have noted elsewhere, one person's difficulty is another's business opportunity. There are lots of people in gainful employment dealing with compliance issues.

This book might give the impression of businesses carefully deliberating about their future courses of action. In practice much IS and IT development work is dictated simply by the need to comply with the regulations imposed by governments. There is, as there has always been, scope for picking a business jurisdiction for your business which has less onerous legal requirements. Some reports suggest, for example, that some companies are joining the London Stock Exchange rather than Wall Street in order to avoid the onerous Sarbanes–Oxley requirements (Finch 2006).

However, the UK and Europe have not been short of compliance demands. Financial institutions in Europe are gearing up to deal with the 2010 deadline for the implementation of the Single European Payments Area. The European Markets in Financial Instruments Directive aims to create common rules for cross-border trading. The financial services industry is grappling with the statutory requirements for pensions simplification. Compliance requirements can appear in unexpected places. The Automobile Association's roadside assistance service can be seen as a form of insurance and so the information systems used to administer the scheme have to conform with Financial Services Agency requirements (Friedlos 2006). These compliance demands worsen the existing problems that large institutions have with inflexible legacy systems. For large financial organizations it has been estimated that 70 per cent of IT costs can be traced to system maintenance. Business leaders can be very frustrated with the constraints and demands of legacy systems preventing the development of new applications that can generate value for the business.

ACTIVITY 4.8 DEALING WITH LEGACY SYSTEMS

What approaches, some of which may have already been discussed in this book, can be adopted to deal with the problems of legacy systems?

CONCLUSIONS

James Thompson was a leading American scholar on organizational behaviour in the 1960s, and we are currently seeing renewed interest in his work. He suggested that organizations have some sub-systems that are geared up to deal with the outside world, such as marketing (Thompson 2003, pp. 10–13). These tend to have a flexible outlook to deal with a changing environment. Other sub-systems carrying out more technical processes tend to have a more inward-looking view, focusing on the execution of technical tasks as efficiently as possible. Organizations vary in the balance between the two viewpoints. 'Traditional' IT operations can be easily identified as belonging to the latter category. The pressures that shape the modern business world – such as globalization, the advent of cyberspace and the demands for business flexibility and agility – require at least some IT-centred specialists to pay more attention to the environment in which the outcomes of their work will have to survive.

SELF-TEST QUESTIONS

1. In SWOT analysis which two of the four factors to be considered both relate to the future?

    (a) Strengths and opportunities.
    (b) Weaknesses and threats.
    (c) Opportunities and threats.
    (d) Strengths and weaknesses.

2. Which of the following statements about the relationship between business and technology is, in the opinion of this book, MOST accurate?

    (a) Business needs must always be identified before the technologies to satisfy those needs.
    (b) The examination of new technologies can identify opportunities that a business can exploit.
    (c) Because IT is a cost that does not generate business value its provision should be outsourced wherever possible.
    (d) As change management is a key concern of all IT development projects, business change is best driven by the IT function in an organization.

3. PESTLE analysis is MOST appropriately applied to which of the following?

    (a) The internal state of the business.
    (b) The competitors of the business.
    (c) The environment of the business.
    (d) The risks affecting a particular project.

4. Localization is which of the following?

    (a) Carrying out each production process in the supply chain in the cheapest region for that type of change.
    (b) Locating the core business as near as possible to the main market being served.
    (c) Franchising local branches of a retail business to local owners or managers.
    (d) Customization of a product – particularly software – for a local market.

5. Which of the following is NOT a characteristic of 'innovators' in Everett Rogers' categorization of the adopters of an innovation?

    (a) Introverted.
    (b) Curious.
    (c) Well-educated.
    (d) Sociable.

6. A product can be adopted without consumers having to make large changes to their way of life or working practices. This is an example of which of the following characteristics identified by Everett Rogers as encouraging acceptance of an innovation?

   (a) Compatibility.
   (b) Relative advantage.
   (c) Trialability.
   (d) Observability.

7. An organization may adopt what they believe is an emerging technical standard, but then find that it does not become widely accepted. Which one of the following terms most accurately describes this situation?

   (a) Prior technology drag.
   (b) Lack of compatibility.
   (c) Stranding.
   (d) High transient compatibility costs.

8. Which of the following characteristics of a potential application would discourage use of mobile phones as a method of interfacing with an information system?

   (a) The task to be carried out is time critical.
   (b) The person who is to carry out the task works outside a fixed office location.
   (c) The transaction requires a large amount of information to be communicated.
   (d) A more senior member of staff has to authorize the transaction.

9. Which of the following statements is true? An EU directive...

   (a) Requires member states to enact laws which have a specified effect in some area.
   (b) Is legally binding on all member states.
   (c) Imposes sanctions on a member state that has contravened EU legislation.
   (d) Is only binding on EU officials, including commissioners.

5 Customer Relationship Management

LEARNING OUTCOMES

When you have completed this chapter you should have an understanding of the following:

- what customer relationship management (CRM) is;
- how CRM can be supported by IT;
- how transaction marketing differs from relationship marketing;
- the four pillars of CRM: customer acquisition, customer retention, customer selection and customer extension;
- how data mining can be used to provide a business with information that can be used to make decisions.

INTRODUCTION

In Chapter 3 we explored the idea of the **value chain**. Each business is placed at some point in a value chain and is linked to its suppliers and its customers. In the case of B2B, its customers will themselves have their own customers. At the end of the chain are the final customers, the actual consumers. They are important as the prices they pay provide the finance that makes the whole value chain possible.

Some aspects of the relationship with customers were explored in Chapter 3, such as the way contact between suppliers and the consumer could be mediated through third parties. In the physical world these could be human beings such as sales agents and brokers and in the virtual world of the internet they could be websites such as search engines or portals.

To some extent, in Chapter 3 the consumer was treated as just another link in the value chain. In this chapter, we look at the particular challenges of attracting and keeping valuable customers.

Customers carry out two basic types of business with the suppliers of goods and services. The first are simple, one-off, **transactions**. In a strange country I might catch a taxi from the airport into a town centre. I pay in the local currency and expect never to see the taxi driver again. This is a one-off transaction. Before I took my flight, I visited my local bank to obtain some foreign currency. I did not have to give them any money over the counter for the currency because I have had an account with the bank for most of my life. The buying of foreign currency was just one event in an on-going **relationship** with the bank.

In both examples, there could be circumstances that could make the transaction more or less part of a relationship. In one locality I might always try to use the same taxi firm, because the drivers are always reliable and pleasant. I could have bought my currency from an exchange at the airport.

From the point of view of a business, relationships are valuable as they introduce stability. A rule of thumb in marketing is that acquiring a new customer is typically five times more expensive than retaining an existing one (Kotler 2003). In terms of Porter's five forces model, the existence of a relationship could be a barrier to the customer shifting their business to a competitor. However, not all regular customers may be valuable – some may in fact turn out to be more trouble than they are worth.

ACTIVITY 5.1 TRANSACTIONS VERSUS RELATIONSHIPS

To what extent are the following likely to be relationship-based? What circumstances might make them more or less like a relationship?

(a) **Buying a daily newspaper.**

(b) **Going to the dentist.**

(c) **Buying a new car.**

(d) **Booking a holiday abroad.**

Marketing efforts can be categorized into those that are **transaction-oriented** and those that are **relationship-oriented**. The activities of the second set are motivated by a desire to build up a clientele of valuable customers who are likely to come back to us again and again. The possible strength of such relationships can be placed on an imaginary ladder – see Table 5.1.

TABLE 5.1   *The relationship ladder (based on Payne 1995)*

1	Partner
2	Advocate
3	Supporter
4	Client
5	Prospect

A rather obvious example is a supporter of a professional football club. Football clubs are commercial undertakings and people who go to football matches are paying customers. However, this bland statement does not do justice to the strength of the relationship in many cases between fans and their clubs. There have been cases, for example, where fans of a football club have stood in local elections to promote planning permission for a new stadium.

CUSTOMER RELATIONS AND THE INTERNET

With commerce by means of the internet, there is a tendency for purchases to be transaction-based. The environment of the web, particularly the reduction of **information asymmetry** – where potential buyers lack the knowledge of the market that sellers have – means that purchasers can hunt down the lowest price for a product or service. This may mean that different purchases of similar products at different times could be from different suppliers. Considerations such as the speed of delivery may be unimportant because businesses may have outsourced delivery to the same delivery specialists. Even where I might use a website such as Amazon for buying books on a regular basis, if a cheaper source were to appear there would be little reason not to switch to it.

One benefit of having longer-term relationships with customers is that the business can learn more about their customers. The nature of ebusiness applications does offer some advantages to businesses in this respect. If a customer, even a transient bargain-hunter, buys something over the web, they will have to give the supplier information such as credit card details or a delivery address. This is valuable information for the business – for a start they can use it to see if a transaction is repeat business. In a physical shop where a customer pays cash and carries the purchase out of the shop, this information is missing – hence the almost universal presence of loyalty cards, which, in conjunction with POS equipment, allows a record of all purchases by a customer to be kept.

Where communication with clients is largely via conversation, whether by telephone or face-to-face, it might be thought that the management of customer relationships would be relatively straightforward. Large complex organizations, however, have particular problems. Each time customers contact such an organization they may well get a different member of staff talking to them. The customer's problem may have to be dealt with by a different department which means that the caller has to be transferred. The person dealing with the particular case may be out of the office. Each conversation with a new staff member may require customers to identify themselves and explain again their reason for calling. This type of unpleasant customer experience can be reduced using two complementary approaches. The first is an organizational approach where staff are organized so that they deal with groups of identifiable customers, not particular products and services. The second, technological, part of the solution is to have a CRM system which gives any member of the customer-facing staff details of all the recent transactions and contacts that the customer has had with the business. This strategic approach which uses technology to enable and support organizational improvements is a key theme that runs through this book.

THE FOUR PILLARS OF CUSTOMER RELATIONSHIP MANAGEMENT

In the next four sections we are going to examine what may be seen as the four pillars of CRM.

- **Customer acquisition.** This is getting the customers in the first place.
- **Customer retention.** This is keeping your customers once you have got them. A general rule of thumb proposed by Newell (2000) is that typically 50 per cent of customers that have been acquired are lost within 12 months and 20 per cent of the remaining customers are lost in every following year.

> ## ACTIVITY 5.2 ESTIMATING LOSSES THROUGH CUSTOMER ATTRITION
>
> A travel agency has just been set up. It is estimated that the average customer of a travel firm will spend £1,000 a year. It is also projected that on average 100 new customers will be attracted each year. Calculate, using Newell's rule of thumb, how much money will be lost through attrition over the next three-year period.

- **Customer extension.** This is trying to get existing customers to buy more. It is known as trying to increase share of wallet.
- **Customer selection.** This is tied up closely with the concerns of customer retention and extension. It identifies those customers who are most profitable. Businesses do not want to spend valuable resources on trying to nurture low-volume customers who may in any case be volatile in their purchasing loyalties.

Having looked at these aspects of CRM, we will pay particular attention to the way corporate decision-making can be improved through the application of **data mining**.

CUSTOMER ACQUISITION

Online versus offline

While some businesses only sell via the internet – Amazon is an obvious example – many businesses have both an online and offline presence – high street banks are examples of these. The internet can be used to promote sales where the actual purchase takes place in a shop or sales room. These shop-sales could be where purchases are very frequent and small and driven by an immediate demand, as in the case of soft drinks such as Pepsi – see www.pepsi.co.uk. On the other hand, they could be for very large items where physical examination of the potential purchase is desirable as in the case of BMW – see www.bmw.com. For a 'pure-play' ebusiness to get an initial momentum, promotion via 'traditional' channels may be called for – see Figure 5.1.

Purchasing

	Offline	Online
Offline	E.g. traditional retail operation	E.g. initial promotion in traditional media of a new ecommerce site
Online	E.g. the web used as just one channel to promote a brand, e.g. BMW	A 'pure-play' internet-based business

(Left axis label: **Promotion**)

FIGURE 5.1 *Offline versus online promotion and purchasing*

Customer segmentation

Before deciding on the best way to attract potential buyers to your business, which more and more these days means your website, you need first to get a picture of the sort of people who might be typical customers. This is part of a process called **market segmentation**. The aim is to find groups of potential buyers who share common, identifiable characteristics. This helps to get an idea of the size of the hoped-for market. Clearly it needs to be quite large if it is going to generate reasonable sales. On the other hand, the identified segment should not be so big that the group just merges into the general public: that would make it difficult to focus promotion cost-effectively.

Segments can be constructed using a variety of customer attributes. These include the following factors.

- **Geographic location.** A business that delivers locally grown organic produce to people's doorsteps is likely to be interested in customers in a fairly restricted area. On the other hand, ambitious firms with proposals to gain business across a range of countries will need to design their sales approaches very carefully. They may in fact need a different marketing plan for each country.

- **Demographic distribution.** This includes looking at age, gender, income and lifestyle. Business proposals exploiting the recreational and entertainment uses of mobile phones, for example, might be expected to target particularly younger people. Some demographic attributes can be linked to your geographic location: given your postcode I can make approximate but useful predictions about your likely income and social class.

- **Psychographic distribution.** This relates to attributes such as your personality and personal interests, for example being particularly interested in sport, either as a participant or a spectator.

- **Behavioural segmentation.** This relates to your behaviour in relation to the product. For example, some types of event can trigger the purchase of certain goods or services. Mothering Sunday, wedding anniversaries and St. Valentine's Day might trigger the purchase of flowers. Whether they actually do depends on your particular circumstances. Other behavioural attributes would relate to the degree to which a product is used, for example the hours spent playing computer games, or the reasons why a person accesses a website.

The marketing mix

Identifying potential customers leads to the question of how they are to be reached. The outcome of this type of decision-making will be a **marketing mix**. This is the portfolio of methods by which it is hoped to engage new customers. The issues to be addressed here are sometimes referred to as the four Ps – **place, product, price** and **promotion**. A later development has been to add a further three Ps – **people, process** and **physical evidence.**

- **Place.** This is how the product or service is going to be delivered to the customer. If the product has a digital format it could be downloaded online. Other products may need to be delivered to the customer's home. In other cases the purchase will have to be made at a shop. The shop might be owned or franchised by the originator of the products, as in the case of motor cars, or the product may be generally available through a wide range of outlets, as in the case of confectionary or soft drinks.

- **Product.** Harris and Dennis (2002) point out that most sales can be seen as delivering a customer benefit rather than just a product. They use the example of 8 mm drill bits. Here, what the customer wants really are 8 mm holes in some material. Thus the customer – unless they are expert in these matters – wants to know that the drill bit is suitable for drilling in plaster walls, rather than that it is tipped with tungsten carbide. This has implications for the wording of websites.

- **Price.** The tendency for the internet to encourage competition on price has already been noted. Price comparison websites reinforce this. New business ventures in established markets will often have a hard time with prices. One tactic is to offer discounts to attract customers to the new product. Some companies go so far as to have a different, lower, price for new customers than for established ones – but this clearly is not contributing to customer retention. The risk with introductory discounts is that the customers attracted may be mainly opportunists who, when the discount is removed, will search for other lower-priced sources.

Direct price competition can be reduced by making the product unique in some way, perhaps by bundling it with complementary products or services.

The internet may not put vendors at such a complete disadvantage in terms of driving prices down as has been suggested above. While prices are important, customers may not be as price sensitive as might be thought. Baker et al. (2001) report a survey that found 89 per cent of online book-buyers bought from the first website they accessed. For toys it was 84 per cent and music 81 per cent. Baker and colleagues argued that ecommerce does put some powerful tools in the hands of vendors. For example, each product has a **pricing indifference band**, a range of possible price levels within which changes have little impact on buyers. Clearly it is in the interest of vendors to establish what these bands are and to set their prices at the upper end of the band. An advantage of ecommerce is that prices can be changed very quickly. It also makes it easier to charge different customers different amounts. This makes it possible to conduct online tests to identify the prices that will maximize sales and profits.

Market conditions change, so prices need to be continually monitored and adjusted. One way to do this is to observe book-to-look ratios: these are the ratios of the number of actual purchasers of a product to the number who have accessed details. A low ratio of purchases to accesses suggests prices might need to be lowered, while a high ratio might indicate that raising prices would be possible as demand is high. Airline tickets are a good example of where a variable pricing system has been established which automatically adjusts prices according to demand.

- **Promotion.** 'Place' refers to the channel by which the product or service will be delivered. Promotion relates, among other things, to the channels by which the product or service is to be advertised. Where several channels are used, it is important that they are co-ordinated. For example, press advertisements should include URLs. Staff should be warned that there is likely to be a surge of enquiries after a particularly prominent advertisement. The channels used will need to be driven by the analysis of market segments discussed earlier. A key question concerns what sorts of media the target market segments are likely to be exposed and pay attention to.

Of the three Ps that some have added to the four above, **physical evidence** is a challenging one in ecommerce. How will buyers be able to make judgements about the quality of goods and services that are on offer? This has links with the concepts of trust and brand loyalty. The concern for this aspect is seen in the widespread use of testimonials from satisfied customers on websites.

Search engine optimization

Search engine optimization (SEO) refers to the steps that can be taken to ensure that your website gets a prominent position when potential customers use search terms that are relevant to your business when using a search engine like Google or AltaVista. A distinction is sometimes made between **white hat** and **black hat** SEO. White hat refers to acceptable practices, which are often things that you would want to do anyway to make your website easy to access and understand. Black hat refers to practices that try to **game** the algorithms used by search engines in a way that the providers of the search engines regard as unacceptable. Black hat SEO could lead to your website being barred by a search engine provider.

This has become a rather specialist area, but some general principles are clear. One is to make sure that a website is designed to make it easy for the **web crawlers** that comb the web examining and indexing sites to do their job. This involves using text on the site that clearly and precisely describes the nature of the business of the site and having clear links to every part of the site so that they are accessible to the crawlers.

The **PageRank algorithm** originally devised by Larry Page and Serge Brin, who founded Google, is largely based on a voting system where if site X points to site Y, then that is a vote for Y. The vote of X, however, is weighted by the number of sites that point to X. Thus it makes sense for businesses who are partners to come to reciprocal agreements to link to each other. In a particular line of business, there are likely to be specialist directory sites in which a business should make sure they have listings.

Despite the apparent benefits of mutual linking, some marketers are reluctant to have links off their website on the grounds that it works against the general principle of promoting **stickiness**, that is, keeping potential customers on your website. One way to overcome this reluctance is for a business to have an affiliate programme through which other websites obtain a fee for each sales prospect who is directed to the business's site – once again Amazon is the exemplar here. For new entrants to a market, where trust needs to be grown in potential clients, these affiliate programmes can have the advantage of being a form of sponsorship or endorsement, so some care ought to be taken with the recruitment of the first affiliates.

> Stickiness is also used to describe the propensity of people to come back to your website.

Online advertising

New businesses will almost certainly need to spend money making people aware of their presence. This could involve buying advertising on the web. Google AdWords, for example, allows customers to display a short advertisement in the margin of the screen when a user makes a query using particular keywords. A challenge with all advertisements is dealing with the risk that they can have a negative effect if they are perceived as being intrusive and if they prevent people going about their preferred activities in peace. As in the real world, web advertising is best where it is very pertinent to the current interests and preoccupations of the customer – which is why AdWords seems like a good idea – or is engaging and entertaining. Banner advertisements which incorporate some kind of game or puzzle can be successful in this way.

Word of mouth

Word of mouth, whereby people make recommendations to their friends and acquaintances, can have a powerful effect on the sales of books for example. As we saw in the discussion of Rogers' model of innovation diffusion in Chapter 4, some individuals may be particularly influential. **Viral marketing**, which can take a number of forms, is an attempt to exploit this. In a modest form, this might be encouraging and rewarding people who identify others who might be interested in your products or services. Another form is to create an amusing animation distributed by email that people might want share by forwarding to their friends.

Touching again on the idea of building relationships, some businesses have been able to nurture online communities. As Everett Rogers points out, for potential users to make the most of a product, particularly if in some way it is a 'tool', the possession of the product needs to be supported by know-how. This know-how might relate to basic use, but could extend to new ways of enhancing your enjoyment of the product. Having bought a hang-glider and having learnt to use it, the enthusiast might be looking for new places to fly. Online communities can pass on information and suppliers can reap rewards as more use of a product eventually leads to more sales. However, online communities have risks as well, as they can become channels for the expression of adverse comments for your goods and services.

Communities take time to build up, but start-up businesses may be able to use existing communities to make potential customers aware of their presence. This needs to be done skilfully so that the supplier is seen primarily as a fellow enthusiast who has something worthwhile to offer.

CUSTOMER RETENTION

Many marketing authorities draw attention to the principle that the costs of acquiring new customers greatly outweigh those of keeping existing customers – at least there is a good chance you know who your existing customers are. However, it may not be worth making expensive efforts fostering lasting relationships with all your clients. As we noted earlier, some transaction-focused purchasers have no brand loyalty and will always shop around (as urged by consumer experts).

It was pointed out earlier that, in order for relationship marketing to work, it must be possible to identify the returning customer in the first place. The opposite is also true: the customer must also be able to identify some established entity that represents some consistent and largely predictable experience. For most readers in the UK, the word 'Marmite' will bring to mind a clear picture of a product and a specific experience (which you might love or loath). This is the power of the **brand**. Some brands have global presence – will any reader from anywhere not be aware of Coca-Cola?

> ## ACTIVITY 5.3 IDENTIFYING GLOBAL BRANDS
>
> **Identify five product or business brands that you think might be in the global top 20 most valuable brands. Use the web to find current lists of global brands against which to check your guesses. If there are some discrepancies why do you think that this might be?**

The consistent expectation that a brand puts in the minds of customers can add considerable value to a product. In Pickton and Broderick (2001), an assessment of Proctor and Gamble is mentioned which puts a value of £8 million on its physical assets but a sum of £37 million on its value to shareholders. The difference of £29 million can largely be attributed to the value of its brands.

It can be seen why, when extending existing brands to new channels such as the internet or attempting to develop new brands, it is important to take a carefully co-ordinated approach. This can sometimes be frustrating for web designers who may find that corporate policies and processes designed to protect the brand can stifle what they see as their creativity.

We have already mentioned loyalty cards as a means of building relationships. They are useful for tracking the purchases of customers who visit shops. We shall see later that they provide rich information for **data mining**. The risk is that customers see them simply as a way of a getting a discount. Research cited by Newell (2000) showed that, in the UK, 83 per cent of shoppers had a loyalty card, but 24 per cent had still switched the main shop they used in the last year; 53 per cent of shoppers had two or more cards and 40 per cent did not think that they were worthwhile. It seems that the secret of successful loyalty cards is to make the 'rewards' rather special such as, for example, something that the shoppers might regard as a desirable luxury but not what they would normally buy for themselves.

The concept of the loyalty card can be transferred to ecommerce where frequent buyers can register via the website and their customer behaviour can then be tracked over time. Where internet users do not identify themselves in this way a website can track repeated visits by the same user by means of **cookies**, small records left in a dedicated file on the user's machine. The website can search for records of previous visits by the current user in the cookies file.

However, customer data collection is only a secondary aim: the main aim is to keep existing customers. Two additional interlinked techniques are commonly adopted to promote stickiness: personalization and customization.

Personalization is tailoring web content for an individual user. It may be as simple as addressing the returning customer by name. An online home delivery supermarket site can allow a previous shopping list to be retrieved, amended and then resubmitted. Where the pattern of a customer's purchases is known, the system can make recommendations based on their revealed preferences.

A risk with personalization if it is applied clumsily is that a user may feel that it represents an intrusion into their privacy: the 'big brother' element might be a little disturbing for some.

Customization is where the users themselves can control the nature of web content. For a news-based website, they might specify that the weather forecast is for the area where they live, the sports results for the sports they follow or the stock market prices for the companies in which they have shares.

Both personalization and customization create barriers to customers switching to other providers of services or goods as it would involve extra work for customers to arrange things according to their preferences in a new environment.

Where the relationship between the customer and a business is a rich and well-established one, the business may be able to detect transactions, for example a change of address, which suggest that a client might be at risk of taking their custom elsewhere. This can be used to trigger activity aimed at encouraging customers to stay with the current provider. This might involve identifying a new branch in the locality where the customer is moving and getting the branch manager in the new locality to introduce themselves to the customer.

CUSTOMER SELECTION

If information on the sales transactions of each customer is being collected, it is possible to analyse the data to identify both the most and the least profitable customers. One way of doing this is **monetary decile analysis**. The value of sales is totalled for each customer. These customer sales totals are sorted into descending value order. The customer sales totals for the top 10 per cent of customers when sorted by value are totalled, the next 10 per cent and so on. A Pareto effect can often be found where, for example, the top 10 per cent of customers are responsible for 30–40 per cent of the value of sales.

> Pareto was an Italian economist and sociologist who noted the tendency for a small number of people to own most of the wealth in a society.

ACTIVITY 5.4 MONETARY DECILE ANALYSIS

Table 5.2 shows that value of sales via a website for each customer for the last month. Carry out a monetary decile analysis on the data, identifying the individual customers and the overall value of sales in each decile when the data is ordered by customer sales values.

TABLE 5.2   *A month's sales figures by customer*

Customer identifier	Sales value £ per person	Customer identifier	Sales value £ per person
a	20.00	k	4.50
b	100.00	l	12.00
c	25.00	m	43.00
d	9.00	n	5.50
e	150.00	o	21.00
f	252.50	p	4.50
g	6.00	q	88.00
h	99.00	r	4.50
i	6.50	s	6.60
j	11.50	t	5.50

When this analysis has been completed, Newell suggests that three main bands of customers can be identified:

- **The most profitable (usually the top 10 per cent).** The priority here is customer retention. As you are probably getting most of their business already, your concern is to make sure that remains the case.
- **The remainder of the top 40–50 per cent.** The emphasis here is on customer extension. This means trying to get the customers to buy more. This might, for example, involve making sure they are aware of the full range of merchandise that you have on offer.
- **The rest.** While these customers may be profitable, they are probably only marginally so. It is probably not making any special efforts for this group.

In some extreme cases, business have actually closed the accounts of customers they have found unprofitable (e.g. FedEx – see Newell 2000). Banks, in particular, may find themselves in a position where the better-off customers may effectively be subsidizing some smaller account holders. However, **lifetime customer value** also needs to be considered – a low-value customer now (such as an impoverished student) may in time develop into a very valuable customer as their circumstances change.

CUSTOMER EXTENSION

This is encouraging existing customers to purchase more goods and services. One approach to this is **cross-selling**. Customers for a particular offering can be made aware of other, complementary, products. Selling travel insurance when someone books an air flight ticket is a prime example of this. The computer system used to record sales transactions can be programmed to suggest complementary items for each sales product.

Data held about a customer may be able to identify key events that provide opportunities to sell new services, for example getting married, having children and retirement. A risk is that too frequent contact can be irritating or even repellent – sometimes a customer can feel they are effectively being punished for providing a business with their custom.

DATA MINING

The motivation for data mining

Marketing decisions are inherently risky. A major reason for this is that a successful outcome for a decision depends on many factors that are outside the control of the business. These risks are especially great when a business proposal relates to a completely new product, the demand for which is very uncertain. Given these uncertainties, marketing decisions need to be made on the best information available.

This information in the strict sense is different from data. Data is the raw, unprocessed material from which information is extracted and refined. A key attribute of good information is that it should be **actionable**, that is, it should be possible to use it to make decisions about future actions. **Data mining** is a term that is used to describe the processes by which raw data can be processed to produce actionable information.

As we will see there are several hurdles that an organization will have to overcome to use data mining successfully. However, some developments have contributed to a growing interest in data mining techniques.

- As we have seen, developments such as the increasing prevalence of POS equipment and the execution of business transactions via the internet mean that more data is being held in an electronic form that allows computer processing.

- Methods of analysing and finding patterns in large data sets have been developed and been made available commercially.
- Computing power and data capacity have expanded and are continuing to expand, providing the means of processing the mass of electronic data available using computationally sophisticated techniques.
- Developments in information systems – including the widespread adoption of ERP systems which is explored in the next chapter – mean that data from different applications but relating to the same entities can be integrated more easily.
- Pressures are increasing to compete more effectively in the market place and to achieve cost reductions by managing value chains more efficiently.

Data mining can be carried out in three different modes: **hypothesis testing, directed knowledge discovery** and **undirected knowledge discovery.** These three approaches are dealt with in the next three subsections.

Using data mining to test a hypothesis

Someone has an idea for some business initiative. The probability of the activity being a success depends on the assumptions made. In a CRM environment these assumptions could well be based on how customers are likely to react. For example, it could be assumed that customers who currently buy a certain product would also be likely to buy a complementary product if it were offered to them. Data mining can be used to test whether the data about past transactions supports this assumption.

Directed knowledge discovery

With hypothesis testing someone has an idea about the factors influencing a particular outcome. In the case of directed knowledge discovery, the aim is to put aside preconceived ideas and to analyse the data to see what factors seem to influence a particular outcome. For example, an analysis might be made to see what factors seem to indicate that the customer of a bank might be about to move their account.

Undirected knowledge discovery

In this case the objective is to get a better picture of the general nature of a data set. For example, if the data is related to customers, it might be useful to see whether there are clusters of customers who share attributes. This would help identify a market segment that might require a tailored CRM approach.

ACTIVITY 5.5 IDENTIFYING A CUSTOMER SEGMENT

Berry and Linoff (1997, p. 81) describe an undirected knowledge discovery exercise conducted by a telephone company who identified a group of subscribers who had a high long-distance call usage most of the year which dropped off dramatically for periods at certain times, especially during the summer and around Christmas and Easter. The group as a whole scored low on several different tests of probable creditworthiness and profitability but was, it turned out, both profitable and reliable. Identify a group of telephone users who might have this profile.

Data mining methodologies

Berry and Linoff (1997) identify a basic methodology for data mining which at the highest level has the following steps:

(i) identifying the problem (or opportunity);
(ii) analysing relevant data;
(iii) taking action;
(iv) measuring the outcome.

They point out that while steps (ii) and (iv) can be carried out by data mining or statisticians, steps (i) and (iii) are essentially business processes. Step (iii), in particular, would in most cases need high-level management support. It can be seen that a close and committed relationship between the analysts who extract actionable information and the managers who direct business operations is a prerequisite to the effective exploitation of data mining.

Data mining and data warehouses

It is not absolutely essential that data mining be based on the existence of a data warehouse. Data warehousing is the process of bringing together in a compatible format data from disparate sources within an organization in order to support decision-making. Data mining can still be carried out without a central repository of data, but this would be much more time-consuming as data may have to be collated by hand after having been extracted from a number of different systems which might have incompatible formats.

The creation of a data warehouse is not a trivial undertaking. Some reverse engineering may be needed to understand the structure and meaning of the data held on different systems. There are bound to be some items of data that are duplicated across systems. These items may be crucial as they may be the keys that allow information from different applications to be linked and combined. Unfortunately it is often the case that what is essentially the same information may be held in different formats and using different coding structures in different parts of the organization and its systems. Considerable effort is often needed to overcome these obstacles.

We have already mentioned the need for data mining experts, who are likely to have a statistical background, to interact with business executives who influence decision-making. The data warehouse brings in another type of specialist: the database administrator whose background is IT.

Data warehouses are not only used by data miners. The data in them can also be used by staff at an operational and tactical level. To make this access easier for staff in a particular function, they may be provided with a subset of the data – a **data mart** – in a structure that fits their view of the business.

What this demonstrates is how data mining and data warehousing are not simply technical matters. They raise many issues at an organizational level and require staff with very different backgrounds to work together if the most effective use of the data assets of a business are to be successfully exploited.

SELF-TEST QUESTIONS

1. An IT consultancy specializes in helping clients configure and implement OTS packages that have been developed by XYZ. Which of the positions on the relationship ladder listed below would the consultancy most likely be at in relation to XYZ?

   (a) Prospect.
   (b) Client.
   (c) Supporter.
   (d) Partner.

2. A study in the south-east of England found that women and those of both sexes under 30 years of age were most likely to buy flowers for Mothering Sunday. Which type of segmentation would this be?

   (a) Geographic.
   (b) Demographic.
   (c) Behavioural.
   (d) A mixture of the above.

3. A technical publication about industry standards in building work is being marketed. The options of selling the publication at normal bookshops or at builders' merchants, by post or by web download, are being considered. To which one of the four Ps of the marketing mix is this decision primarily related?

   (a) Place.
   (b) Product.
   (c) Price.
   (d) Promotion.

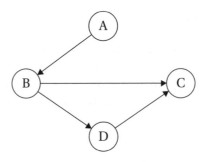

FIGURE 5.2 *Website linkages*

4. In the diagram in Figure 5.2, the nodes A, B, C and D represent websites. An arrow between two websites indicates that the first one contains a URL pointing to the second, for example A calls B. Which of the four nodes is likely to have the highest ranking using a basic PageRank algorithm?

(a) A
(b) B
(c) C
(d) D

5. Which of the descriptions below most accurately describes directed knowledge discovery in data mining?

(a) Gathering evidence to check that an idea is valid.
(b) Analysing data from different sources with a view to integrating them.
(c) Analysing data to see which factors have an influence on an outcome.
(d) Detecting patterns or clusters in a data set.

6 Enterprise Resource Planning Systems

LEARNING OUTCOMES

When you have completed this chapter you should be able to demonstrate an understanding of the following:

- the roots of enterprise resource planning (ERP) applications in the needs of business for integrated information systems;
- the essential characteristics and potential of ERP systems;
- ERP system implementation strategies;
- ERP and BPR;
- exploiting ERP: the introduction of strategic enterprise management systems.

INTRODUCTION

In previous chapters the focus has been on the use of ebusiness applications to communicate and co-ordinate activities with other businesses in the supply chain, and also to nurture lasting and profitable relationships with customers. We have looked at the links between the business and its suppliers and customers but not at the processes inside the business that support these outward-facing activities. For example, a B2C web application that allows customers to place orders online would soon collapse if sales thrived but adequate systems had not been set up to update inventories, place orders to maintain stock levels, process customer payments and organize deliveries. These types of transaction are just some that would be processed by means of an **enterprise resource planning** system. An ERP system is essentially an integrated set of applications supporting business processes with a single unified database. As Koch et al. (2001) say:

> 'Enterprise resource planning software, or ERP, doesn't live up to its acronym. Forget about planning – it doesn't do that – and forget about resource, a throwaway term. But remember the enterprise part.'

Because of this potentially confusing name, some prefer to refer to **enterprise systems**. We will stick with ERP as this is the name that is so commonly used and also, as we will see, it is in the longer term useful to remember the 'resource' and 'planning' bits.

Most businesses are likely to have a core of basic systems that are common. Of course, such differences as do exist could be very important as it could be these that give the business its distinctive character and competitive edge over its rivals. Despite this most businesses have similar core systems – see the list in Table 6.1.

TABLE 6.1   *Examples of common business-wide systems*

Sales orders	Payroll
Customer billing	Financial accounting
Purchase orders	Distribution
Stock control	Accounts payable
Accounts receivable	Personnel records
Bank reconciliation	Assets management

These almost universal applications that allow businesses to operate tend to be quite intimately linked. This might be illustrated by the extremely over-simplified model in Figure 6.1 which shows just some of the functions that would need to communicate with one another in a wholesale business. Co-ordination would be needed so that, for example, the warehouse always had enough stock to satisfy orders, but not too much so that money was spent unnecessarily on stock gathering dust on pallets in the warehouse. There would also be a question of financial control. We would need to know, for example, the value of sales orders and the costs incurred in satisfying those orders in order to assess the on-going financial viability of the business. An information system, whether primarily computer-based or clerical, would be needed to provide this information.

In the simplistic example illustrated by Figure 6.1, a process is triggered when a customer places an order with the sales department. The sales department would have to check with finance that the customers are creditworthy before passing the details of orders to the warehouse so that the right goods can be picked and dispatched. If the items required are not in stock, the sales department would have to be informed so that they can notify the customer and perhaps try to persuade them to take an alternative product. If the order can be satisfied, a delivery is scheduled and the dispatch note sent with the goods to the customer is copied to finance. Finance can then raise an invoice which is posted to the customer.

ACTIVITY 6.1 FUNCTIONS OF A WHOLESALE BUSINESS

We have said that the model in Figure 6.1 is simplistic. In what ways might the real-world system be more complicated?

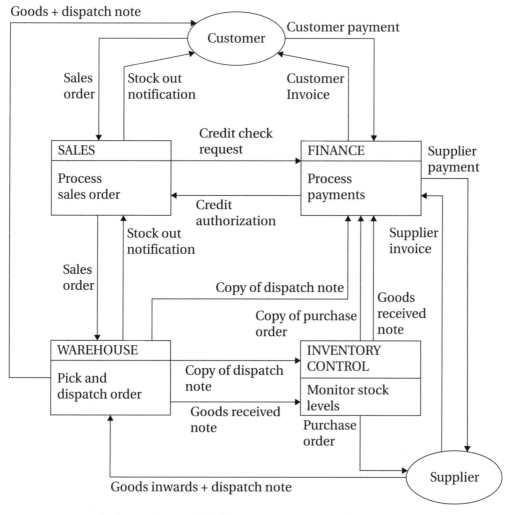

FIGURE 6.1 *Functions of a simple wholesale business model*

This process affects three functions directly: sales, the warehouse and finance. Another, inventory control, is involved indirectly. In the early days of 'electronic data processing', there was a tendency for computer applications to be developed for single functions which had exclusive use of their own data files. Where data had to be transferred between these systems it was often done by means of one application generating a file of data changes that were then used to update the other application through the execution of a batch operation, usually carried out overnight. Sometimes businesses had to resort to the manual re-inputting of printed reports to transfer details. Integrated applications which could share common data stores would avoid such tasks and thus the idea was developed of the **corporate database**, which held in one place all the data stored and used by an organization. In the 1970s and 1980s time and effort was spent by businesses and other organizations in drawing up corporate data models that aspired to document all the data needed for the day-to-day operations of a business and also for longer-term planning. Early attempts at building systems which supported and exploited such corporate databases usually met with little success. Partly this was because the technologies available at the time were not up to meeting the physical demands of such applications. A database structure could often be optimized to provide a reasonable performance for a single application, but it was usually difficult to deal with several applications which had conflicting processing needs. Another problem was the huge amount of development and organizational effort needed to develop a whole range of applications, serving all aspects of a business, which were to work together.

At the same time, another major impediment to progress was making itself felt more and more in the world of business IT. This was the **legacy system**. These were core IT systems that were crucial to the operation of the business. Typically they ran on large mainframe computers. They were often the original 'killer app' that had justified the organization adopting IT in the first place. As key applications they were often the first to be developed and so they tended to be written with a lack of experience and expertise compared to later systems. As the years passed, the application software had been changed time and time again to deal with new, often externally imposed, requirements. The more that software is modified, the more it becomes unstructured (or 'spaghetti-like') and more difficult to amend. The staff effort required to maintain legacy systems often sucked away development resources and thus impeded major new IT developments. Over time organizations had come to depend hugely on these monsters.

> Here we talk about legacy systems in the past tense, but many are still with us today.

The last straw for many organizations was the **Y2K problem**. In retrospect, it seems incredible that so much time and expense could have been spent on what now seems such a trivial problem. It will be recalled that the problem was that many computer systems held dates in some form of 'YYMMDD' format where only the last two digits of the year were recorded. The advent of the year 2000 meant that, for example, calculations of the number of days between two dates in different centuries (to check whether a payment was overdue for instance) would not work. (Some commentators suggested that truncated dates stemmed from the need for early computers to save computer memory space – as a programmer at the time I can only testify that this was not the case: there were many ways of holding compressed dates which could have avoided this problem.)

> We realise that some claim that 2000 was the last year of the 20th century rather the first year of the 21st century!

The adoption of ERP systems was seen by many organizations in the 1990s as a way out of this mess. The ERP solution came from an unlikely source. One area where integrated computer systems had had some success from quite early on was manufacturing industry. A significant problem for some manufacturers is planning production when they win a major new order for a product. One aspect of this is ensuring that the raw materials and components needed to satisfy the order are available when needed. A **bill of materials** is rather like a list of ingredients for a recipe. It records the amounts of each raw material and the numbers of each component needed to create so many units of a particular product. In some cases components have to be assembled from sub-components. In fact, it is possible for a complex product to have several such levels of subassembly. Having identified the lowest-level components and raw materials, current stock levels have to be checked, orders placed to remedy any shortfalls and the dates identified when, as production progresses, further orders would have to be placed. These kinds of calculations were ideal for computer automation, and so a class of software – **materials requirements planning (MRP)** – was developed in the 1970s for this role. As time went on additional factory forecasting applications were built, for example, to extend planning to staffing and finance, and a new generation of more sophisticated software emerged in the 1980s called **manufacturing resource planning** or **MRP II**. A further development was to extend the range of integrated business applications even further to cover all the main operations of the business and the concept of ERP software emerged. The coining of this term is attributed to the Gartner group in the 1980s.

It was noted earlier that despite its name ERP does not seem to have that much to do with the process of planning. We can now see that the 'planning' element came from its MRP origins. The principle of using data about new developments to forecast future repercussions should be kept firmly in mind when considering how to get the most from ERP.

ACTIVITY 6.2 FUTURE REPERCUSSIONS OF CURRENT EVENTS

What future events and actions can be predicted from the following? Think about the short-term consequences and also the longer-term ones as the effects of a sequence of similar events are accumulated:

(a) someone accepting a job offer;

(b) receiving an order from a domestic consumer for a product;

(c) an increase in the price of an important component of a popular product;

(d) an employee handing in their notice;

(e) a unit of equipment used in a manufacturing process needing repair.

One of the characteristics of this new breed of business applications was that they tended to be supplied off-the-shelf by external suppliers. The supplier that became prominent in the 1990s was the German company SAP AG. SAP was founded in 1972 by five former IBM employees and originally stood for *'Systemanalyse und Programmentwicklung'* (Scapens et al. 1998). These days SAP is said to stand for 'Systems, Applications and Products in data processing'. The R/2 system, launched in 1979 (the 'R' stands for 'real-time'), was based on mainframes and had the modules shown in Table 6.2 (Keller and Teufel 1998, pp. 67–101). R/3 was introduced in 1992 and was based on client–server architecture.

TABLE 6.2   *Examples of SAP application modules*

Module	Example content
Financial accounting	General ledger accounts; accounts receivable; accounts payable; legal consolidation; asset accounting
Investment management	Capital programmes and measures; depreciation simulation
Controlling	Overhead cost controls; product cost controls; profitability analysis
Sales and distribution	Sales; shipping; billing; sales support; sales and distribution information
Materials management	Materials requirements; purchasing; inventory management; warehouse management; invoice verification; logistics information
Production planning	Sales and operation planning; master planning; materials requirements planning; capacity planning; discrete and continuous order processing
Quality management	Quality planning; inspections; quality control; quality certificates; quality notifications
Plant maintenance	Service management; preventive maintenance; maintenance management
Project systems	Planning; budgeting, execution; project information
Human resources	Organizational management; personnel development; workforce planning; training and event management; recruitment; time management; incentives; payroll; travel

Client–server technology was a great enabler for ERP. Being able to distribute the processing between a central server and scattered clients made remote access easier. This architecture allowed the acquisition by user organizations of commodity hardware units. A commodity product is a standardized unit that can be used in a number of different environments and can be manufactured by a number of different companies. Standardization and universal applicability increase the opportunities for sales. This, in turn, allows economies of scale to reduce production costs.

Along with competition between different suppliers this helps to drive down costs. The modular nature of client–server architecture also facilitates the scaling up of systems as new applications and their users are added. As Vogt (2002, p. 63) noted *'It was client/server technology systems that boosted ERP systems, and made the boom…possible'*.

In the 1990s, businesses which were facing the Y2K problem and felt that they were constrained by their legacy systems found ERP applications to be a very attractive proposition.

THE CHARACTERISTICS AND BENEFITS OF ERP SYSTEMS

Most of the distinguishing characteristics of ERP applications have been touched upon in the last section, but it is convenient to summarize them at this point. An ERP system has the characteristics listed below.

- It is a comprehensive and integrated set of IS applications covering the key business transactions of an enterprise.
- Information and data are held in a common integrated database.
- Data is updated in 'real-time', that is, as events trigger transactions. This is particularly important where a transaction in one application – such as a sales order – has to update details belonging to another application – such as the stock levels held by an inventory system. Overnight batch updates of data in associated systems are eliminated.
- The core ERP software is supplied by an external party, a specialist supplier of OTS ERP applications. It is possible for part or all of an ERP application to be developed in-house by a user organization, but this does rather undermine the business case for the business change and carries with it a number of risks, as we will see shortly.
- Because the ERP software is almost invariably provided by an external supplier, the nature of the functionality is largely predetermined. It can only be altered to fit local user requirements at some cost and difficulty. The predetermined functionality is based on a **reference model** which, the suppliers claim, represents identified best practice in respect to a particular application.

In the 1990s, the major ERP suppliers, apart from SAP, included J.D. Edwards, Baan (a Dutch company which tended to supply systems for smaller enterprises), Oracle and Peoplesoft (which had originally focused on human resources systems before extending their product range to other ERP applications). Since 2000 there has been consolidation: J.D. Edwards merged with Peoplesoft in 2003 and in 2004 it was Peoplesoft's turn to merge with Oracle. Baan has merged with SSA Global. Since 2000, the Sage group, Microsoft, Siebel, Geac, Intenta, Info Global and Lawson have all emerged as significant ERP suppliers. SAP, however, continues to dominate the market.

THE MOTIVATION FOR ERP ADOPTION AND ITS CHALLENGES AND RISKS

The adoption of ERP applications has some clear benefits. The fact that they are usually provided by external suppliers means that they have all the advantages – and disadvantages – normally associated with OTS software. The software should, for example, be cheaper than in-house development as the development costs are spread over many customers. Software which has already been in use for some time with a large number of users is also likely to be more reliable as this pool of previous users will have effectively debugged the system. The software will be ready for use after configuration – a process which admittedly might not be completely straightforward. The users of software that is being specially written would have to await the completion of its development. They would also have to carry out rigorous testing to ensure that the previously unused software was sufficiently reliable. ERP applications would need some testing but this would not focus on the correctness of the underlying software but on the way it was to be installed in a business.

The implementation of an ERP system should have the benefit of incorporating an integrated database shared between the different 'modules' in the ERP portfolio of applications. A common database would ensure the removal of duplicated data leading to more efficient and consistent processes. It should contribute to better data quality: for example, if the address of a customer changes, the change will only need to be recorded once and all users of any of the associated ERP applications will have access to the new address. This ease of data access means that business processes can be speeded up. A sales clerk dealing with a new order for a customer can immediately access customer details to check their credit rating and access the inventory to check the items required without having to request the information from other departments. This improved data access at an operational level could be matched by the ability of managers and financial controllers to extract more up-to-date and coherent management information from the corporate database.

The management of an enterprise may be motivated to adopt an ERP system as it gives them the opportunity to organize their business processes more efficiently. The standardized reference model which governs the way that the ERP system has to be used can enable a backward business to adopt what is recognized as 'best practice'. In some mature and complex industries, work practices may have evolved over time in a piecemeal manner leading to there being parallel processes with the same purpose but different mechanisms. These processes would benefit from consolidation and standardization. An example of this, described in Schneider (1999), was Boeing which at one time had amassed a large number of legacy systems, including 450 which fed into the production process. There were 14 different bills of materials systems and 30 shop-floor control systems. The same details often had to be input into a number of different systems with the inevitable transcription errors and inconsistencies.

The need to introduce common company-wide systems has been a strong incentive for the adoption of ERP. A business may have a number of different and incompatible sets of processes in different locations because it has evolved through the merging of formerly independent businesses. The introduction of ERP may be motivated by a simple desire to impose a common system on the consolidated business so that a consistent and coherent financial picture of the organization as a whole can be extracted and presented. Fahy (2001, p. 128) provides a case study based on Thermo King (Ingersoll) involving the roll-out of an ERP system to sites in the USA, Spain, Germany and Ireland. The new system speeded up the business's financial processes, particularly where in the past details had to be extracted from incompatible legacy systems. The business change project allowed the production of important financial summary information to be produced much more quickly.

A further advantage of ERP adoption is that businesses can take advantage of the new applications as ERP suppliers extend the functionality of existing modules, for example by adding web-enabled supply chain management (e-SCM). The fact that many businesses have the same ERP applications will make it easier to implement these interorganizational systems. In fact, some smaller businesses have felt compelled to adopt ERP systems in order to be able to do business with more powerful customer organizations who have them already. As Shehab et al. (2004, p. 359) have commented:

> 'ERP is now considered to be part of the price of entry for running a business, and at least for the present, for being connected to other enterprises in a network economy....'

It is clearly in the interests of the suppliers of ERP systems and services to publicize ERP successes. It does no harm to the staff in the client organization to have people know about their achievements. Fahy (2001, p. 15) contains a report of an unnamed supplier of computer-aided design software that, through the installation of an ERP system, was able to reduce the delivery time for orders from an average of two weeks to one day. Another report indicates that the introduction of ERP allowed Allied Signals' turbo charging unit to improve its on-time delivery rate from 65 per cent to 92 per cent (Fahy 2001, p. 104), while one Boeing plant was able to reduce costs by 25 per cent, improve the on-time delivery rates from a range of 65–75 per cent to one of 85–95 per cent (Fahy 2001, p. 103). Chevron Corporation reported cutting purchasing costs by 15 per cent. IBM Storage Products reduced the time needed to change price details from five days to five minutes (Beynon-Davies 2002, p. 167).

Finally Autodesk Inc. claim to have saved enough through inventory reductions to pay for their entire ERP implementation.

However, the complete picture has not been that rosy, so that for example one survey showed that less than 30 per cent of the responding organizations had achieved the expected benefits of ERP. There have been some well-publicized ERP disaster stories. The Hershey Food Corporation in 1999 had major problems with meeting the orders for its confectionary products, especially during the run-up to Halloween which, in the US, is period of high demand for sweets. The problems were blamed on software faults in newly installed ERP modules and the users' lack of familiarity with the new systems (Vogt 2002, p. 65). Among other ERP disasters, the FoxMeyer Corp. drug distribution company in 1996 blamed being forced to file for bankruptcy partly on the failure of an ERP implementation (Vogt 2002, p. 66). It is probably true that no ERP implementation is easy, but a common theme with these mega-disasters is that often the problems did not stem from the use of well-established ERP modules, but from the development of brand new software components. Often this was because ERP applications were being developed in business environments where the existing ERP functionality was not appropriate. In this light ERP disasters often look very similar to traditional software disasters.

The factors affecting ERP success can be usefully divided into those that relate to **business design** and those that relate to **implementation**. The next section will look at the business decisions that will have to be made, while the one following that will examine implementation issues.

STRATEGIC DECISIONS WITH ERP

Davenport (1998) presented a useful overview of the possible business advantages and risks of ERP and the strategic decisions that management teams would have to consider. These decisions may be more finely balanced than some enthusiastic descriptions of the benefits of ERP might suggest. Davenport gives several examples of businesses that have made huge improvements by standardizing procedures throughout the different divisions of their organizations. However, it remains the case that if all the businesses in a sector are pursuing similar strategies, then competitive advantage might lie in doing something different. For example, the success of a business could well have come about through the building up of relationships of co-operation and trust with customers over a substantial period of time. Davenport gives an example of a spare parts service that consistently gets parts to its customers 25 per cent quicker than its competitors. It does this partly by circumventing formal processes. Perhaps, for example, it is prepared to deliver spare parts on the basis of a simple phone call without having to wait for formal paperwork. A more formal, standardized, system might be more 'rational' but less effective. Another example might be an e-procurement system where business buyers have to use authorized suppliers from an official list. This could mean that buyers could not take advantage of local knowledge that might be able to identify cheaper local sources of goods and services.

Where some business units are based abroad, a competitive edge might be lost because foreign business practices which are at variance with local expectations and customs might be imposed on local business partners and customers.

Davenport identifies the following types of strategic decisions that need careful consideration:

- federalism – the degree to which the centre imposes common processes as opposed to local variation;
- the selection of ERP modules to be installed;
- the scope for customized application components;
- overall business value.

Federalism

Davenport argues for the consideration of a **federalist** approach where a careful analysis distinguishes those areas where standardization and consolidation have business value, as opposed to those areas where local differentiation and customization will reap benefits. One consequence of this might be that differently configured ERP systems would be implemented in different divisions of the same organization.

Selection of ERP modules

Careful thought also needs to be given to which modules in an ERP portfolio are to be implemented. The example of Elf Atochem North America is cited where only a subset of SAP modules that dealt with the major concerns of their business change strategy were implemented. These were just the modules that dealt with materials management, production planning, order management and financial reporting. These processes were the focus of an organization-wide initiative to streamline 'end-to-end' business processes that had previously been disrupted by different functional units having different responsibilities and interests in the same transaction.

Customization

We have already touched upon the substantial risks involved in developing your own ERP components. Sometimes, however, the business benefits of developing a software asset that your competitors have not got might be worth the risks. Compaq is given by Davenport as an example of where the business realized that forecasting the demand for products and managing orders were crucial processes in their drive to build products only when triggered by orders rather than to create stock in the hope of future sales. This motivated the business to design and write their own software to maintain competitive advantage in these key operations.

Business value

In the section that follows about implementation issues, it will be seen that the costs of ERP implementations can be enormous and also that the pay-off from the implementation will probably not be immediate. In this situation, it could be that competitive advantage could go to the businesses that do not undertake such major expense and disruption. Air Products and Chemicals is a company that decided that its current systems were adequate to meet its needs and that the cost of the massive changes that ERP entails could lead to them having to increase prices to customers.

The management team of the business thinking about adopting an ERP implementation will need to consider the longer-term risks of being locked into a single supplier of enterprise software. The major investments that a company will have made in their ERP systems and the degree to which they affect almost every aspect of the business would discourage most businesses from completely replacing their ERP systems once installed. Porter's five forces model would suggest that this is a barrier to change that would give the supplier a strong hold over captive clients which could be exploited, for example by increasing licensing fees over time.

ACTIVITY 6.3 APPLICABILITY OF ERP SYSTEMS

Explain the degree to which an ERP solution is likely to be helpful in each of the following scenarios.

(a) Two financial organizations are being merged. Each has its own systems which have largely been developed by internal development teams, although in recent years the proportion of costs going into support and maintenance has tended to increase at the expense of new development. The intention is to merge the systems of the two organizations.

(b) A business organization has grown by buying up smaller businesses in a variety of specialist and retail areas in a number of different countries in Europe, Australia, the Indian sub-continent and the Far East. There is a large degree of local management autonomy. Quite often less well-performing units have been sold off.

(c) A business employing about 30 people provides specialist services, conducting geological surveys of sites selected for building projects. It has a substantial number of large clients. At present, payroll and accounting functions are carried out by an outside service bureau. There are some software applications that have been written by a contract software developer which are used to schedule jobs and record survey data.

As we will see shortly, a further concern would be the **degree of fit** between the suppliers' offerings and the way the organization currently does its business. While some of the application modules may be ideal from the business's point of view, others may be less suitable. In this case the opportunities for mixing and matching modules from different suppliers would need to be explored.

THE ERP IMPLEMENTATION PROCESS

To appreciate the challenges of implementing ERP systems, you need firstly to be familiar with the stages that an ERP implementation would go through. As will be seen, there are some important differences between some of these stages and those in the conventional software development life cycle. Although ERP is clearly an IT or IS application, the involvement of the IT and IS functions of an organization could be relatively modest in relation to the size of the development. It could be largely limited to overseeing the provision of the underlying IT infrastructure.

We will go through the typical stages of any ERP project, using a case study of an ERP implementation at Seimens Power Corporation to illustrate certain points (Hirt and Swanson 1999).

Project evaluation

Any substantial business change project will need to be justified. Usually this is done in a document that lays out the business case for the development. In the case of the SAP R/3 implementation at Siemens Power Corporation (SPC), the decision to adopt an ERP solution resulted from a report by consultants on the restructuring of the business to regain its market position. One recommendation was to discontinue using an IBM configuration on the grounds of cost (a saving of US$800,000 a year). Other identified savings were based on reducing duplicated effort by replacing separate application packages with an integrated ERP-based system.

> The possible content of an evaluation report will be explored in Chapter 7.

Project preparation

A project team and a project management structure will need to be set up. Compared to a conventional IT system implementation, a majority of the team members could well come from the business and user communities within the organization.

Requirements gathering

Analysis will focus on the business needs that the proposed business changes should satisfy. This activity could identify weaknesses where current processes need to be changed. Alternatively it may find that current business practices are so important for competitive advantage that the customization of the software would be justified.

Package and vendor selection

Note that not only will a software vendor need to be selected, but also a source for any new hardware platform upon which the ERP software will run. Because of the complexity of the process of configuring ERP applications, it is usual practice to employ systems integration specialists who have expertise in the selected package.

> ### ACTIVITY 6.4 PACKAGE SELECTION
>
> **Identify the main activities involved in package selection.**

Technical architecture and design

The decisions made here include how the ERP applications are to be integrated with the other systems in the organization. In the case of SPC, it was decided that permanent interfaces would have to be built between the SAP modules and some of the existing applications at SPC such as payroll, freight-billing and production scheduling.

The business change team must also decide how existing business data will be transferred to the new computer systems and how clerical systems will be converted to the new work practices.

Other important strategic decisions will be confirmed at this point. One of these will be whether to have a **big bang** change-over to the new system or whether to go for the **phased** approach. In the case of SPC, the system integrator recommended a big bang change over. As its name perhaps suggests, a big bang approach – where a change from one system to another takes place over night – is inherently risky. It can, however, be quicker and less costly than transferring systems one at a time. The extra costs of the incremental approach come from the need to build temporary interfaces between ERP modules and old systems the functionality of which is yet to be transferred. There can also be what has been called **software breakage**. This is a result of the later increments generating new requirements in ERP modules that have already been installed. Another disadvantage of the incremental approach is the increased risk that consultants may leave before the implementation is completed.

In the end SPC went for a three-phase transfer, essentially because they did not have enough staff to deal with one huge peak period of work.

Implementation analysis

The integration analysts conduct workshops with knowledgeable user representatives, or **super-users**, in order to get an understanding of the current procedures. The key concerns here are the differences between the current work practices and the package's way of working. Hence this is sometimes called **fit-gap analysis** – or **as-is analysis** as the focus is on what the current systems do.

Configuration

The analysts now set the parameters to configure the package. This is often done in two steps. In the first, analysts build a **baseline** version of the ERP module using the findings of the fit-gap analysis. The analysts and super-users then **walk through** typical transactions to check the compatibility of the system with the current company practices. Where there are discrepancies, adjustments could be made either to the system configuration or to clerical procedures.

In the SPC case study, some people at SPC felt that having two separate stages of implementation analysis (IA) and configuration was unnecessary. One manager was quoted as saying:

> 'We spent a lot of money on the IA. It did not get us any closer to installing the software and of getting it up and running. It got me a lot further along in my expense column.'
>
> Hirt and Swanson (1999, p. 248)

Testing

It could be argued that as the software has already been heavily used in previous installations, the kinds of bugs that can beset newly written software should not be present and thus testing can be minimal. However, the amount of parameter setting involved in configuration and the integration of different aspects of the client's business that have perhaps previously been fragmented means that testing is crucial.

Training

ERP system implementations are about changing business processes. For the end-users and their managers it can mean that a completely new way of working is to be introduced. Boersma and Kingma (2005) quote a chief information officer on the organizational impacts of an ambitious ERP implementation at Nestlé:

> 'no major software implementation is really about software. It's about change management.... When you move to SAP, you are changing the way people work....You are challenging their principles, their beliefs and the way they have done things for many, many years.'

Thus training is essential to the success of the implementation. It can be advantageous to use the super-users who acted as user representatives and experts in the local business processes as the lead trainers. Users will want to know about using the new system in the context of their daily work and the super-users understand their world. Users are also more likely to trust those who they can regard as their own people – see the discussion of the work of Rogers (1983) in Chapter 4.

Data migration

The database of the new system will need to be populated with data that was previously held on the old system. It may be that one-off software applications will have to be written to transfer the details or that even, in extreme cases, there may have to be staff actually keying in details. Many applications now have facilities to download and upload data in spreadsheet format from their databases. This allows data from one application to be modified by hand in spreadsheet format so that it is acceptable for uploading to another. A moment's thought should suggest that such operations are risky and that careful reconciliation of the data on the two systems is required.

A challenge is that the details may have to be **cleansed**. Some records may be found to be 'dead' – they may for example hold details of products that have long since ceased to be sold. The more intimate the integration of systems the more important the accuracy of data will become. To take a small example, in one invoicing system the invoice records held the job reference for the work that was being billed. However, this was only used occasionally by billing office staff to resolve queries. The accuracy of the job reference was not therefore seen as crucial. However, in an integrated system, the job reference was used as a database link to the work management system and carelessly entered job references for a time became a headache.

Post-implementation support

Our own discussion with staff who have been involved with ERP implementations (e.g. Hughes et al. 2002) confirms what even the staunchest advocates of ERP systems have to concede – for example (Fahy 2001, p. 76) – that immediately after implementation productivity may actually go down as users try to get to grips with the new ways of working. At this point user satisfaction with the system is going to be particularly low: to quote a project manager in the SPC scenario, '...*the users hated the system because it was so hard to understand*' (Hirt and Swanson 1999, p. 250). Where there has not been the opportunity for a lot of user training then users might be given lists of instructions that they have to follow in an apparently mindless way in order to get things done. To quote the same source, '*sometimes we had to tell them to do it by rote. You need to know that if you want to place an order, this is what you have to do.*' This approach, which may be forced on an organization by necessity, will inevitably lead to large numbers of queries when things go wrong or when slightly non-standard situations arise. Staff knowledgeable in the new system need to be on hand to help users. At first many of the problems will be trivial, but when more major problems occur it may be that the 'experts' cannot initially come up with a quick solution as they too are learning how to cope with the new system.

A key lesson is that while some enthusiasts may claim that there will be immediate returns on investment, most of those who have experienced ERP implementations warn not to expect too many dividends in the short term.

STRATEGIC CHALLENGES WITH ERP IMPLEMENTATIONS

Figure 6.2 is a causal map (Eden et al. 1992) which illustrates some of the issues that affect the success of ERP implementations. Each hexagon represents a **concept variable**, that is, a general condition or factor that has a value in a range between two opposite extremes. Thus one of the these concepts variables *'able to change software…unable to change'* is a condition which has one extreme of being able to change the software with complete ease and another where the functionality of the software is unchangeable. Between the two there is a range of possible values reflecting particular circumstances. The arrows between the variables represent cause and effect. This suggests, for example, that a decision to change the software of an ERP system (*'customize software… not'*) will be influenced by both the degree to which making such changes is easy and the size of the gap between current business processes and the reference model of the ERP system (*'large …. small gap between business and ERPS'*).

This map suggests that there are five main variables that affect the implementation strategy for ERP:

(i) the efficiency gains that will come from improved IT support, for instance real-time updating and an integrated database;
(ii) the ease with which software can be customized to deal with local requirements;
(iii) the degree to which the previous business processes at the recipient organization match those in the reference model upon which the ERP application is built;
(iv) the ease with which the current business processes can be modified;
(v) the degree to which it is perceived that there are benefits in changing the current business practices.

The model suggests that there are two key sets of decisions that affect ERP implementations. One set arises from the degree of misfit between the current business applications and the expectations of the ERP application as documented in its reference models. The greater the degree of misfit,

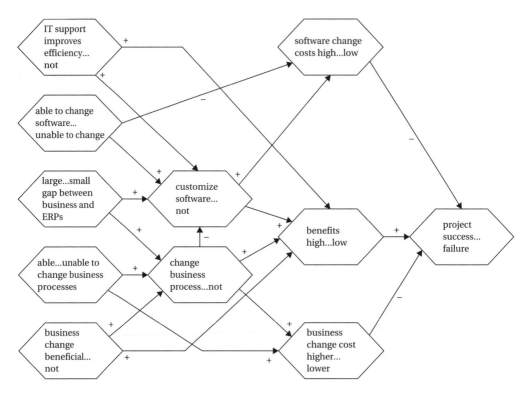

FIGURE 6.2 *Causal mapping of ERP implementation success*

the more problematic the implementation – this is discussed in more detail in the next section. The second set of decisions relates to how misfits can be dealt with. The options are to try to change the software or to change work practices. This decision will be influenced by the ease of customizing the software and both the ease and desirability of changing business processes.

ACTIVITY 6.5 ERP SUCCESS FACTORS

Given the model in Figure 6.2, what might be the likely outcomes in the two project scenarios?

Factors	Project A	Project B
IT support improves efficiency…not	low	very high
Able to change software…unable	very low	very high
Large…small gap between business and ERPS	high	low
Able…unable to change business processes	high	high
Business change beneficial…not	high	low

PACKAGE–PROCESS MISFITS

A highly recommended source here is Soh et al. (2000) who examined the implementation of ERP packages at seven public hospitals in Singapore. Although the research related to a very specific set of circumstances, some very useful and generally applicable principles were identified by the research.

The research identified three main types of discrepancies between the administrative processes of the hospitals and the demands of the ERP package. These were those relating to **data, functions** and **outputs**. Within each of these major groupings, some further sub-headings emerged. Table 6.3 uses the classification of Soh et al., but we have substituted our own examples.

In addition to the classification of misfits, Soh et al. (2000) also identified a spectrum of misfit resolution strategies, some of which tend to a greater or lesser extent to change the way the organization works. Other strategies move in the opposite direction of customizing the ERP package – see Table 6.4.

TABLE **6.3**   *Package–process misfits*

Misfit type	Explanation	Example
Data – format	The data format used by the package does not match that used locally	Formats of dates and postcodes
Data – relationships	The way that different items of data are linked together	The systems may insist all payments have to be associated with an invoice. Business practice has been to allow payments against a customer account without an invoice
Functional – access	Differences in practices about who has access to what information	Clerical staff have access to customers in their designated region only. This constraint is not supported by the ERP package
Functional – control	Differences in validation rules	UK postcodes different to US zipcodes
Functional – operational	Differences in business rules	Calculation of local taxes
Output – presentation format	Layout of reports etc. makes it difficult to use in the local situation	Accounts in account number order, whereas clerks access by name
Output – information content	Local requirements need information not provided by the system	Government requirements for information from local authorities

TABLE 6.4   *Misfit resolution strategies*

	1	2	3	4	
Organizational change	Change organizational procedures to match those of the ERP system	Accept a shortfall in ERP – reduce scope of requirements	Devise 'work-arounds' or alternative ways of carrying out required functions	Customization of ERP package	ERP customization

Workarounds might be either changes to clerical processes, using alternative features of the ERP package or a mixture of both. **Customization** might involve **non-core processes**, for example developing an add-on software component, or using a report-writer feature of the package to extract information from the database. Alternatively it might involve changes to the core code of the application. The implications of this are tackled in the next section.

THE ISSUE OF FLEXIBILITY

The last section identified some of the ways by which an ERP implementation team might try to bridge the gap between local working requirements and the constraints of an ERP package. It can be seen that much depends on how flexible such a system is. For example, to get most benefit, businesses might like to have the option of getting different applications from different vendors – a '**best of breed**' or **BoB** approach. Different vendors have different reputations: Boersma and Kingma (2005, p. 128) noted, for example, that SAP was regarded as particularly good on financial management, Baan was seen as good for logistics and Peoplesoft for human resources. Creating links between the offerings of different vendors, and between vendors' systems and systems developed in-house, could require the development of custom interfaces.

Specially developed interfaces may be particularly vulnerable when a new version of one of the portfolio of applications is released by the vendor and adopted by the organization. New releases are not always simply new versions with a few changes, but can sometimes be substantial reworkings which require significant modifications to interfaces. As a consequence, a new breed of software, **enterprise application integration (EAI)** products or middleware has been developed to deal with these problems of interoperability.

Sometimes EAI is called AI (for application integration) which is confusing.

We have so far spoken of the integration of applications inside an organization, but the need to communicate and interoperate with the systems of business partners is becoming increasingly important. Bahli and Ji (2007) describe an interesting case study where a business that provided global IT support sold off one of its divisions. The services of what were now units in different organizations were distinct but inter-related, so that customers would often require the services of both businesses to deal with different aspects of the same job. Also the two businesses carried out work for each other in their respective areas. It therefore made sense for them to have access to each other's CRM systems, but the two organizations used different CRM applications which led to the unnecessary tasks of keying the same details into both systems. An EAI system was installed which, it was reported, allowed the response time for dealing with customer calls for help to be reduced from five working days to six hours.

> Recall from the last chapter that CRM stands for customer relationship management.

The need for flexibility and the ability to integrate applications has led to some developments in methods and technologies, in particular the structuring of software applications into **components** which provide services that can be called upon by a range of applications. This is in contrast to monolithic and self-contained applications where data might only be transferred to other applications via feeder files – and even that option might not always be available. It has always been possible for software to be modularized so that calls could be made to standard components to carry out commonly required procedures such as calculating the number of days between two dates. The mechanism for doing this was usually for a copy of the segment of software code to be incorporated into the application. If a change was made to the master copy of the software component – to correct a fault, for example – a new copy of the code segment would have to replace every single old copy of the segment in the host applications. It would be more convenient for a single, free-standing, component to be called up when needed. An organization might, for example, have several separate applications which manage the provision of different types of goods and services and each might call upon a billing system to issue an invoice.

The advent of the web has allowed this concept to be developed further into **web services** where the common functionality can be situated on a different platform accessed via the web (Sprott 2000). Some competing software standards have been developed to enable this approach, notably COM, Enterprise Java Beans and CORBA.

ERP AND BUSINESS PROCESS RE-ENGINEERING

One motivation for the acquisition of ERP, noted earlier, was that it might provide opportunities to re-arrange work practices in order to make them more efficient. In these cases there are, theoretically, three options:

(i)   to re-engineer the business processes before the adoption of ERP;

(ii) to re-engineer at the same time as taking on ERP;

(iii) to install the ERP system and then streamline the clerical procedures afterwards.

It is probably true to say that users prefer the second option as the others would involve two upheavals rather than one. However, it is argued that getting the best value from ERP requires the initial installation to be just the start of a continuous programme of process improvement. Martin and Cheung (2005) provide a useful description of one such process improvement initiative at Mobil Oil Australia.The development in question was the result of a global initiative to streamline the accounts payable process. The time-honoured way of placing an order and its subsequent processing include the following steps:

(i)   a request for an order to be placed is made by a member of staff;

(ii) a manager approves the order and it is passed to the purchasing department;

(iii) the purchasing department selects a supplier, issues a purchase order to the supplier and sends a copy of the order to the accounts payable section;

(iv) the supplier delivers the goods which triggers the generation of a goods received note (GRN) which is passed to the accounts payable section;

(v)   the supplier also generates an invoice for the amount due and sends that to the accounts payable section;

(vi) an accounts payable clerk checks the prices on the invoice against those on the original order, and the amounts delivered against the GRN. If everything is consistent then the invoice is paid.

This process may appear to be long-winded. However, while the originators of the order may sometimes be frustrated as they may not be sure what is happening with their orders, at least responsibility for the administrative processes is devolved to someone else.

In the Mobil scenario, the simple expedient of introducing corporate credit cards helped simplify the ordering process. For orders up to a certain limit, an authorized staff member could phone the supplier directly, place an order and quote the credit card number. The supplier delivered the goods or provided the services. Then they claimed the amount due via the credit card provider. The accounts payable section was only involved when the credit card provider issued the monthly statements and the payment of the balance on each card had to be authorized. The manager (who was also a budget-holder) of the employee who had made the purchase would receive a copy of the monthly statement that they would need to scrutinize.

While this reduced the work that the accounts payable section had to carry out, it had certain costs. The 'empowerment' of individual employees and their managers meant that they had responsibilities they had not had before.

Under the new arrangements, orders above a certain limit had to go through a more formal procedure. Stage (f) of the original process – see above – was, however, slimmed down. Rather than the accounts payable section checking invoices against the original purchase order and GRN, delivery of the goods ordered triggered the creation of an invoice in the Mobile system on behalf of the supplier based on the unit price on the original order and quantity delivered. Cash transfers were then automatically generated. Invoices from the supplier were simply ignored.

The savings from these and other associated changes to processes allowed Mobil Oil Australia to reduce accounts payable staff from 19 to five people. However, as noted earlier, this was not without costs. The 'empowerment' of staff and managers in operational departments meant that their responsibilities increased – for example, they had to answer queries about payments from vendors, whereas before the accounts payable section would have dealt with this. There was also a weakening of controls and an increase in opportunities for buyers to breach internal organizational standards. It would be interesting to know to what extent individual departments had to set up their own local record keeping in order to maintain an up-to-date picture of their own expenditure.

STRATEGIC ENTERPRISE MANAGEMENT

In the Mobil Oil Australia case study, processing was reduced by eliminating some controls felt not to be cost-effective. The reduction of internal control is not, however, a universal feature of ERP systems. Once an integrated set of communicating applications is in place, it is possible for the ERP system to extract operational data from key points in the end-to-end processes. This data can then be used to provide an up-to-date picture of the performance of operations.

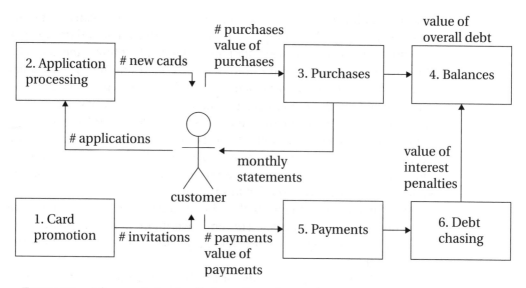

FIGURE 6.3   *A fragment of a simplistic credit card operation. Note: # stands for 'number of...'*

To take a very simplistic example. Figure 6.3 represents some possible elements of a credit card operation. If this is an integrated operation, the number of letters sent by the marketing department to prospective customers inviting them to apply for the card could be counted (process 1, *card promotion*). The number of actual applications that result from process 1 can be counted in process 2, *application processing*. Comparing the two counts provides an indication of the effectiveness of the marketing campaign. Process 2 would also provide counts of successful applications. If a large number of applications are rejected, this might suggest that the marketing operation needs to be more selective in targeting prospective card users. Details of the number and value of purchases by card-holders would be key indicators of business health – money is made by charging commission on sales. Sales might be expected to be in step with seasonal and economic cycles and trends, but if the number of card-holders increases but the number and value of purchases remains static, then this might suggest a need to stimulate purchases, perhaps through a points scheme. The credit card provider also makes money from charging interest on the balances carried over from one monthly statement to the next, so the difference between the value of purchases and payments needs to be monitored. While large balances may be good news as interest charges increase, debts that are too large might make the company vulnerable through bad debts.

> This is a grossly simplified model that, for example, ignores the role of the retail outlets.

An integrated system where the key performance indicators are extracted at vital points in the processes could clearly help overall control of a business. In some cases it might be possible to link these indicators to some form of employee incentive scheme. However, there is a risk of **sub-optimization:** a local process might be energized by incentives – for example, dramatically increasing the number of applications. However, this might be to the detriment of other parts of the business. For example, credit card applications may overwhelm the department that deals with applications. An increase in applications might result in more acceptances, but this might be because creditworthiness criteria are weakened leading to more bad debts.

The general principle here is summarized by Fahy (2001, p. 148):

> *'If a company can understand and model the dynamics of the business and the cause and effect relationships, it can use these to identify key business drivers.'*

Another variation on this theme is the advocacy by management accountants of activity-based costing (ABC). A vital decision for businesses is setting the prices for the goods and services that it supplies. On the one hand, it will be influenced by competitive forces – as was seen in Chapters 2 and 5. The more competitive the market, the lower the profit margins that can be maintained. A danger is that for a particular product or service the price is actually less than the costs. The reader may think that situations where particular products and services are generating losses would be obvious to all but the most incompetent business executive. However, there may be cases where profits on one product are subsidizing losses on another closely related product. This may not be easy to detect because it may be difficult to link some business costs to specific products. More accurate costing might help eliminate unproductive lines and boost overall profitability. As an ERP system can integrate data from different stages of the business's internal value chain, it can track across a number of processes the costs related to a particular job or product. This can provide a platform upon which ABC and activity-based management (ABM) can be based.

> The emphasis on allocating costs to product lines needs to be balanced by the idea of core competencies that can support several different products – see Chapter 2.

ABC can be seen as a method of extracting detailed and precise information from operational systems which can be used by managers to make tactical and strategic decisions. Another aspiration is for management information systems to be built that can give top-level management an aircraft cockpit style display which can summarize the current state of a business. The concept of the **balanced scorecard** has been advocated by

Kaplan and Norton (1992). This summarizes the state of an organization by extracting and displaying a set of key indicators relating to broad areas of concern. Our personal experience has been that the aspiration that such scorecards should be generated automatically from operational data is very problematic. Sometimes the statistics displayed, say by an impressive intranet interface, are actually created by clerical effort using spreadsheets. Different parts of the business are likely to work to differently timed cycles – for example, human resources data is likely to be less volatile than daily sales figures. Where the results are being used to judge the performance of the middle managers, then some indicators may refer to conditions over which managers in fact have very little control. For example, if a business is instituting a redundancy programme the line managers probably cannot do much to stop surveys showing declining levels of staff job satisfaction.

SELF-TEST QUESTIONS

1. Which of the following is most likely to be a valid reason for adopting an ERP system?

   (a) To speed up business processes by the use of IT with a minimum of disruption of day-to-day business operations.
   (b) To allow different business applications to share data.
   (c) To gain competitive advantage by having IT-enabled processes that are superior to those of competitors.
   (d) To boost the business's financial position by an immediate reduction in operational and support costs.

2. Which of the following MOST closely describes what is meant by a reference model in the context of ERP implementations?

   (a) A process model of the way an organization currently works and which any IT system will need to support.
   (b) The structure of the documentation that supports and describes an ERP system.
   (c) The configuration of clerical and automated processes that will be in place after ERP implementation.
   (d) The business processes assumed by an ERP application.

3. Which of the following MOST closely matches what Davenport calls federalism?

   (a) Each division in a business decides for itself whether to adopt a particular ERP module.
   (b) While other, non-IT, business decisions are delegated to organizational divisions, the use of the ERP is mandated by the centre.
   (c) Divisions have their own IT systems but use common systems to communicate with one another.
   (d) The centre identifies situations where standardization through ERP would reap benefits as opposed to local differentiation.

4. Which of the following MOST accurately explains the meaning of the term 'software breakage' during a phased implementation of an ERP package?

   (a) The configuration of later modules requires changes to modules already installed.
   (b) The installed ERP application works in a way that is incompatible with the business processes of the organization.
   (c) Incompatible settings during the configuration process cause failures during operational running.
   (d) The data passed from a vendor-supplied ERP module to an application developed in-house has incompatibilities that lead to in-house software having to be changed.

5. Which of the following is a good reason for a phased approach to ERP implementation?

    (a) Internal staff effort is dispersed over time.

    (b) Overall costs will be less.

    (c) There is less chance of suffering from staff departures.

    (d) It is likely to lead to fewer changes to systems.

7 From Ebusiness Strategy to Implementation

LEARNING OUTCOMES

When you have completed this chapter you should be able to demonstrate an understanding of the following:

- how a business proposal is assembled;
- the options available to implement an ebusiness proposal;
- the financial indicators used to assess the economic viability of a business development proposal;
- programme as opposed to project management;
- the importance of benefits management.

INTRODUCTION

In this chapter we try to bridge the gap between the development of the business idea and the turning of the idea into a business reality through its practical implementation. Firstly we will expand on what we mean by 'strategy'. Next we will explain how a business proposal is assembled. This will link back to the material presented in previous chapters. It will show how the results of the various analyses described in those chapters can be brought together to create a coherent business proposal. The next part will then introduce some new analytical techniques and implementation options that may need to be considered when building a business proposal.

The final major topic of discussion is the way that a major business or IT change might need to be implemented through a series of projects that are co-ordinated as a **programme**.

THE REAL NATURE OF STRATEGY

Elsewhere we have argued that the viewpoint of IT practitioners tends to differ radically from that of business strategists (Hughes et al. 2006). IT practitioners are usually concerned with the creation of 'technological objects' which are deterministic in nature. By 'deterministic' we particularly refer to the expectation that IT systems should work according to precise, agreed, specifications. At the level of business strategy, business leaders and the analysts who might advise them are dealing with broad decisions about future actions where the outcomes are uncertain. The nature of the decisions at this higher level is usually 'political' to a greater or lesser degree – and the word 'political' is not being used in a pejorative sense. The journey from broadly stated aims which can be fulfilled in many different ways to IT and IS applications that tend by their very nature to be complex and inflexible is bound to be difficult.

To many the term 'strategy' suggests some carefully concocted master plan where every future move by an organization has been thought through and orchestrated in detail. Indeed some major engineering projects might aspire to this model. As many management gurus such as Tom Peters (1988) have pointed out, in a rapidly changing environment longer-term plans are likely to very rapidly become obsolete. The late Claudio Ciborra studied the way technology-based organizations such as Olivetti actually developed strategically (Ciborra 1996). He found that the strategy of such organizations was often largely improvised. He used the French word '*bricolage*' to refer to the makeshift improvisations by which many organizations progress. It could be argued that such improvising simply reflects the way poor organizations operate and that with the most effective organizations things are very different. It just so happens that most of us personally have never actually worked for such well-organized companies.

Rather than denying that such improvisation takes place in success-ful organizations, some management writers (going back at least as far as Quinn 1980) have explored the idea that successful organizations have found ways of improvising that tend to lead to desirable outcomes. Ralph D. Stacey (1993) summarized this approach with the following points.

- Such strategic management is not piecemeal. There is a clear view of the destination of the business.
- Although the destination is clear, the pathway to that destination – that is the 'strategy' – is not predetermined. There is an awareness of the uncertainties of the larger world which means that the way of reaching the desired destination may change.
- The actual strategy emerges through the interaction of a range of people in the organization who have different needs and levels of influence.
- *'The result is an organization that is feeling its way to a known goal, opportunistically learning as it goes'* (Stacey 1993, p. 264).

A risk with such an approach is that it can become simply reactive. If nothing prods the business to change then the chances are that it will never change. Some initiatives are needed to work proactively towards the long-term objectives. However, some of these steps may be tentative. For example, several different products may be developed. Some may sell well while others may not. The secret is to be able to move quickly to exploit the successes fully and to limit the damage of the less successful initiatives.

David Feeny (1997) makes broadly similar points to Stacey but examines the specific situation of IT investment. He identifies six characteristics of a 'business-led' approach to IT investment and implementation.

- The starting point should be a business problem or opportunity which if successfully addressed should bring a real value to the organization. You do not start with the current IT capabilities or business practices.
- The business owns the development. Different functions will contribute their own specialist expertise.
- Managers will need to get away from day-to-day operational demands in order to have time to think about and contribute to new developments. Feeny refers to the need for an 'away-day' culture.
- Some high-level modelling techniques such as those discussed earlier in the book, including Porter's five forces analysis and SWOT, can help structure collaborative thinking.
- The development team will be able to call on the services of other specialists both inside and outside the organization.
- The result is *'an integrated design for a new business initiative, which spells out requirements for IT as well as other functional areas'* (Feeny 1997, xxiv).

The approach as described above does not, by itself, preclude the creation of grandiose, monolithic and ultimately ineffective strategic plans. However, Feeny promotes the idea that the objective should be to produce a sequence of relatively quickly delivered benefits rather than have a monolithic project that might take years to implement. He uses the image of *'dolphins, not whales'*, where there are frequent and brief immersions in technological and business change, interspersed by periods of coming up for air. We will return to this idea later in this chapter where we discuss an implementation approach based on programmes of projects rather than individual projects.

The need for IT to be shaped by business identified by Feeny is a sentiment that is frequently echoed. To be fair to IT practitioners, if they had to wait for a lead from their business colleagues, in some cases they would have to wait a long time. Many organizations are poor at developing new opportunities as they are preoccupied with the resolution of daily operational issues. Not spending time on longer-term thinking is often justified as a focus on the customer, and longer-serving employees may recall gone-by grandiose strategic plans and programmes that have subsequently petered out.

Despite this, clearly some longer-term thinking is essential if new business opportunities are to be exploited. Some have argued that what is needed to promote longer-term thinking is a **business analyst role**. This would act as an intermediary between the business and IT function. These analysts should take both the high-level aspirations and the detailed practical concerns of the business and translate them into technical requirements that IT specialists can understand and implement.

APPROACHES TO BUSINESS ANALYSIS

The introduction of the role of the business analyst is one attempt to create bridges between the business and the IT function. The translation of business needs into technological requirements is a key organizational activity that is fraught with difficulty. One aspect of this is the premature selection of a technical solution to a business problem. An analogy can be made to natural language translation where a hazard is that a word that in one language has a very restricted meaning can be used to translate a word with a much broader range of meanings in another language. Similarly, there may be a range of options available to satisfy a business need. However, the requirement may be communicated to the IT development and implementation teams in a way that implies a single, very constrained way that the business need can be met. This may be just a symptom of a broader problem. A project manager of our acquaintance who works in the financial services industry has observed that many people feel more comfortable dealing with changes to existing systems than being given a relatively blank sheet of paper upon which to suggest requirements for a completely 'green field' application. This unease is understandable as the best solution in such circumstances is not obvious as there may be so many uncertainties. A danger is that people jump at the first plausible option that appears (rather than the best one) in order to quickly move the discussion to a level of practical detail with which they feel comfortable.

This is just one way people within organizations deal with the difficulty of a blank sheet of paper. We have also identified the following tactics.

Adapt and extend existing IT systems

This is a focus on the adaptation or extension of existing IT systems rather than on the creation of completely new ones. When this policy is pursued purposefully then the ethos could be one of continuous evolution.

The main risk associated with this approach would be a growing reliance on legacy systems. These can be constraints on progress as they are costly, risky to change and also require specialist staff familiar with the systems. As more and more changes are made to the same software, the structure of the system becomes more difficult to change. At some point a strategic decision will have to be made whether to replace the application rather than amend it further. A purely financial analysis would balance the cost of replacement against the possible reductions in maintenance effort. Very often, however, replacement is forced upon an organization because of the obsolescence of the hardware or software platforms that support application.

Computerization of existing clerical procedures

This is the 'traditional' approach to systems analysis, embedded in methodologies such as SSADM, the structured systems analysis and design method formerly sponsored by the UK government, which carefully document the existing processes in a system. Usually the focus is the analysis of processes currently carried out manually, but could include currently automated processes. The result of this analysis is a logical, or conceptual, model of information processes in the current system. It represents the processes 'logically', that is, it does not take account of the physical means by which the data is held or is processed. A computer-based system is then constructed which is at least partially an automated version of the logical model. The translation process does not have to reflect slavishly the preceding logical system as process improvements may be identified. This approach will not work where there is no existing clerical equivalent of the new application. This will often be the case with ebusiness proposals.

Analysis of system objectives

Here the focus is on the meeting of system objectives. In the UK, this established systems approach is particularly associated with Peter Checkland (Checkland 1982, Checkland and Scholes 1990, Checkland and Holwell 1999), but is part of a broader systems tradition. The initial assumption is that the true purpose of a purposive system would be a transformation of some form of input into outputs. However, the system could be dysfunctional where there is a contradiction between what the actual outcomes of the system are and what they should be. The result of the initial analysis is a **root definition** that defines the core purpose of the system in terms of this translation of inputs into outcomes. A **conceptual model** is then created. This shows the activities needed in an ideal world for the purpose of the system described by the root definition to be fulfilled. As this approach was designed by systems specialists they put great store on some activities existing to monitor and control the conceptualized system.

As an example, a chain of department stores decides to expand their business to accept orders from customers via a website. The goods will be delivered to the customers' addresses. A very simplified root definition could be the transformation of customer orders into delivered goods. From this the conceptual model shown in Figure 7.1 might be generated.

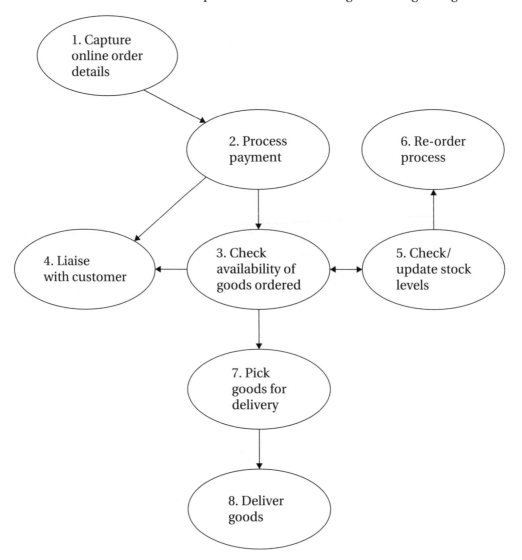

FIGURE 7.1   *A conceptual model*

The activities in the conceptual model are then taken in turn and current operations are examined to see to what extent they carry out the processes needed by the activity. Where there are gaps or deficiencies in the current operations then the development of new processes is indicated. For example, activity 1, 'capture online order details', would be a completely new process. If the department store already had a mail order service, then activities 5, 6, 7 and 8 would probably already have processes in place which could be used. On the other hand, if home deliveries were not currently catered for, then arrangements for such deliveries would need to be put in place.

ACTIVITY 7.1 DRAW UP A CONCEPTUAL MODEL

Draw up a conceptual model of a process that transforms a requirement for work to be done within an organization into newly recruited members of staff. Explain the nature of each activity in the conceptual model.

Focus on building working models

Where potential users of the new system have difficulties grasping how they might use it, simulations or prototypes could be developed that allow the users to experience the form the new system might take. The prototypes might be **throwaway** which are discarded once they have been used to elicit the users' requirements. Alternatively, an **evolutionary approach** may be adopted where the prototype is refined, through a number of revisions, into the operational system. The principle of prototyping is particularly appropriate for ebusiness applications as they often have a direct interface with the business's customers and there is also often no existing clerical system on which to base the new system.

Benchmarking

Comparisons can be made between the performance of a business and other businesses of a similar type. Where the other organization seems to have superior technologies or processes these might be copied. Detailed information about the internal processes of direct competitors may be difficult to obtain. In this case organizations similar in structure but in different, although comparable, markets may be more willing to provide insights.

The vision versus the blueprint

A key point is that, when business analysts negotiate with the customer-facing part of an organization, they need to focus initially on the desired **end-state**. In a later section we will examine a particular approach to programme management that is promoted by the UK Office of Government Commerce (OGC). This methodology recommends the early creation of a **vision statement** which defines the new capability that the proposed business change should give to an organization. When this has been drawn up, the **blueprint** can be drafted which identifies the changes needed to the organization in order to achieve the vision.

A BUSINESS PROPOSAL

Purpose and content

Organizations will have different titles for the document that we call here a **business proposal** such as, for example, a **feasibility study**, a **business case** or a **project justification**. Its key purpose is to justify the start of work on a development project by showing the value of the benefits of the implemented system will exceed the costs of developing, implementing and operating the system.

Business proposals vary in size. They could relate to the launch of a major new step forward for an international company that transforms the way it operates. It could be a proposal to set up a sole trader business employing one person.

Proposals can also be distinguished by target audience. Is it within the organization that employs the proposer? Or is this a pitch for funding to external private investors? This chapter assumes that the proposal is for a new ebusiness capability within an existing organization.

Typically the main sections would be:

(i)   Introduction
(ii)   Background to the proposal
(iii) The new development
(iv)   The market
(v)   Organizational and operational infrastructure
(vi)   The benefits
     (a) Financial
     (b) Quantifiable
     (c) Non-quantifiable
(vii) Outline implementation plan
(viii) Costs
(ix)   The financial case
(x)   Risk assessment
(xi)   Management plan

These sections will now be described in more detail.

Introduction

This explains the purpose of the report. Casual readers picking up the document should quickly find out what it is about by glancing at this section.

The introduction also contains a management summary, a set of bullet points presenting key findings and recommendations.

Background to the proposal

This describes the current environment in which the proposed development is set. Within this environment a problem to be solved or an opportunity to be exploited is identified.

The new development

This describes the new development that is proposed.

The market

This section will be relevant when the proposal concerns a new product or service offered to the public. The market segments should be identified. Potential demand should be assessed and possible competitors noted. The methods by which customers are to be made aware of the offering should be described.

Organizational and operational infrastructure

This will explain the changes to the organizational structure needed to implement the proposal. The changes proposed may affect people's working lives, so this section needs to be carefully drafted to be persuasive.

To illustrate the kind of material that might be included here about the operational infrastructure, take the example of the department store website operation modelled in Figure 7.1 above. As well as the web application the store would need a physical operation that would process orders, pick goods from a warehouse and get them delivered. The ways in which these are to be set up would need to be described. As discussed in Chapter 3, a major issue could be the degree to which processes are carried out in-house or outsourced.

Benefits

Benefits can be of three different types: quantified and valued, quantified but not valued and identified but not quantified.

Quantified and valued benefits

'Valued' here means that a financial value can be assigned to the benefit. Where the proposal is designed to generate money then the revenue model that applies should be identified. In other cases, there may be a financial justification built upon the saving of money. This latter type of financial justification could be used as much by not-for-profit organizations as by commercial ones.

Quantified but not valued

When we say that the benefit is 'not valued' we mean we cannot easily assign a financial value to it, not that it is not appreciated. Where an application is for a public service, we noted above that it is often justified on the grounds that it saves money. However, some applications in the public area are justified on the grounds that they improve the service to the community. For example, in a command and control system that dispatches ambulances to deal with medical emergencies, improved communications and dispatching processes can shorten the time between a call for help being received and an ambulance being dispatched. Statistics can be collected to show that improvements to processes have in fact reduced dispatch times. For this type of measurement to be valid, it must be possible to demonstrate cause and effect between the proposed change and the claimed benefit.

Identified but not quantified

Some claimed benefits may simply be too vague to assess, for example an enhanced public image. In other cases the causal link between the proposed business change and the hoped-for benefit will be too loose to show a correlation between them. An expensively produced website might be able to help increase sales at a chain of shops, but many other factors such as the range of goods on sale, the prices in comparison with rival offerings and the reputation for quality might also influence sales. It is not suggested that non-quantifiable benefits should never be taken into account, only that they need to be considered very carefully.

ACTIVITY 7.2 IDENTIFYING FINANCIAL BENEFITS

Explain the financial value of the following benefits:
  (a) The speedier delivery of goods ordered by customers.
  (b) Delivering recorded music via downloads rather than the physical delivery of CDs.
  (c) The delivery of training material via elearning applications that allow the sales advisers employed by a financial services organization to learn at their own workstations rather than attending courses.
  (d) The use of online advertising which targets internet users who use particular keywords in search engines which suggest they might be interested in your product.

Outline implementation plan

As noted above, the proposal does not concern itself solely with the IT aspects of the business change. Things such as marketing, promotion and operational and maintenance infrastructures have to be addressed by a plan. Key decisions will be which project activities can be outsourced and which are best kept in-house – this was one of the issues considered in Chapter 3. The question of whether an activity should be kept in-house or be outsourced can be asked of both operations and development. With software acquisition, there are a variety of options available which will be compared in the section on 'Implementation issues'.

Costs

Having outlined the steps needed to set up the operations needed by the proposal, a schedule of expected costs associated with the planned approach can now be presented.

There will clearly be some uncertainties about some of the costs. Traditionally, one of the worst areas for estimating errors has been the development of new software. This is one of the reasons why implementation strategies that reduce the amount of new software to be developed to a minimum are often attractive. We would argue that it is often more realistic to provide a figure that is thought to be the most likely, plus positive and negative error margins, for example '20 staff-months of effort, plus or minus 3 weeks'. Note that here we have given an estimate in staff-months that can be converted into a monetary value by applying a monthly rate. That monthly rate would vary depending on how the staff effort is obtained. For example, the use of in-house developers, if they exist, would be less expensive than the use of temporary contractors.

The financial case

The sections of the report on the market and the benefits should have identified the revenue streams and the other sources of value that the proposed application or business change should collect. When it comes to projections of actual sales then the degree of uncertainty can be huge where a product is particularly novel in some way. For this reason we would argue once again that a method of presentation that shows a number of scenarios ranging from pessimistic to optimistic is more realistic than relying on a single forecast.

The section on costs gives us our outlays, and by comparing projected income and costs we can generate a business case for the development's financial viability. Michael Blackstaff's book (Blackstaff 2006) provides an excellent explanation of the principles and techniques involved. One much-used indicator of financial viability is the **pay-back period** which is the length of time the new capability will have to be in operation before the original investment is paid off. The **return on investment** (ROI) is the average annual return on the original amount invested expressed as a percentage. Income that is due in the future is worth less than the same amount in your hand now, as the money you have now can be invested to generate further income. **Discounted cash flow** (DCF) analysis, as will been seen, takes this into account.

In project evaluation the objective is to compare a range of proposals in order to decide which represents the better investment. Different evaluation techniques often come up with different results. It is also usually possible to change the outcome of a model by changing the assumptions upon which the model is based. You should therefore ensure that the evaluation is done in exactly the same way for each of the proposals being assessed.

Whatever analysis technique is used, the starting point is to estimate the income (or savings) and the out-goings for each year in the life time of the project. Here we are using the term 'project' in a rather special sense. It includes not just the development and implementation phases of a business change (which could include the development of a new product), but also its years of operation. Any costs or income associated with decommissioning the project would also be included.

Let us take two business proposals, A and B, the cash flows of which are presented in Tables 7.1 and 7.2, respectively.

TABLE 7.1   *Cash flows for proposal A*

Year	Out-goings	Income	Cash flow	Accumulated cash flow
0	10,000	0	−10,000	−10,000
1	4,000	2,000	−2,000	−12,000
2	1,000	3,000	2,000	−10,000
3	1,000	8,000	7,000	−3,000
4	1,000	10,000	9,000	6,000
Totals	17,000	23,000	6,000	

TABLE 7.2   *Cash flows for proposal B*

Year	Out-goings	Income	Cash flow	Accumulated cash flow
0	10,000	0	−10,000	−10,000
1	1,000	10,000	9,000	−1,000
2	1,000	8,000	7,000	6,000
3	1,000	3,000	2,000	8,000
4	4,000	2,000	−2,000	6,000
Totals	17,000	23,000	6,000	

Here we are using 'year 0' as shorthand for 'all investments made before the new capability became operational'. The cash flow column shows the difference between the out-goings and the income for each year. The accumulated cash flow column shows the sum of the cash flows for the project so far up to the end of each year of the project.

We have contrived the example so that both proposal A and B have the same initial outlay of £10,000 and over their lifetimes will generate a surplus of £6,000 on the original investment.

Return on investment is calculated as:

ROI = (average annual profit)/(total investment) × 100.

Thus for both proposals the ROI would be:

ROI = (6,000/4)/10,000 × 100
     = 1,500/10,000 × 100
     = 15%.

> There are different versions of ROI so care must be taken to calculate it consistently for all the proposals being compared.

There are, however, some striking differences between the two proposals. With proposal A there is considerable expenditure in the first year of operation. This could be the case where there is a need to promote a new product. Once the product has been exposed to the market there is a steady growth in income year on year. With proposal B, it would appear that the product is something for which there is already a high demand. However, once the rather small window of opportunity has been exploited, then income declines rapidly. This might be the case where the product exploits a passing fashion that is then replaced by another. We might at first sight be tempted by proposal A because the income from the development increases steadily as each year goes by. On the other hand, we should be aware that these figures are only estimates. The further into the future we try to make guesses, the more likely those guesses will turn out to be inaccurate.

We could compare the two proposals by calculating the **pay-back** period. The key concern for an organization might be to ensure that we can pay for the development fairly quickly. After that we are happy to have any profits that come our way but we do not have to be too worried about the size of those profits. This might be the case where many of the benefits hoped for are not easily measured in precise financial terms.

We calculate the pay-back period by totalling the cash flows from the start of the project year by year until we find the year the accumulated cash flow figure turns from being negative (that is, we are in debt) to being positive (we are making a surplus). For project A this is 3.33 years and for project B it is 1.14 years.

The fractional element is calculated as:

Pay-back point = $x + (abs(\ acc_x)/cshflw_{x+1})$

where:

x = last year when the accumulated cash flow was negative
acc_x = accumulated cash flow at the end of year x
$cshflw_{x+1}$ = cash flow for year $x+1$.

It can be clearly seen that, according to this criterion, proposal B is superior because large financial benefits are realized early on in the life time of the project. Once the initial development costs have been covered, subsequent income, however large, is ignored.

ACTIVITY 7.3 CALCULATING THE PAY-BACK PERIOD

Purchase and installation of optical character recognition equipment will cost £20,000, but will save £5,000 in staff costs in the first year of operation. In each successive year it is estimated that savings will grow by 10 per cent as the business expands and sales income increases. A contract has been signed for maintenance of the equipment that will cost £750 a year. What would be the pay-back period for this project?

What the pay-back calculation does not take into account is how the investment in the project might compare with putting your money on deposit in a bank or building society. If we have the option of putting our money into an account where we can gain interest, money we have in our hand now is always going to be more valuable than money we are promised in the future. If you give me £100 today and I can get 5 per cent interest, then in a year's time it is worth £105. The £100 that you are going to give me in a year's time is thus the equivalent of having £95.24 today. The interest over a year on that sum would be (at 5 per cent) £4.72 which, if added to the £95.24, would have given me £100 in a year's time. That £95.24 is called the **net present value** (NPV) of £100 in 12 months' time. The NPV is calculated by multiplying the actual income in 12 months' time by 1/(1+interest rate). This multiplier is called the**discount factor**.

To get £100 in two years' time would need an investment now of:

£100 × 1/(1+interest rate) × 1/(1+interest rate)

that is, £100 × 0.9524 × 0.9524, i.e. £90.70.

The calculation of the discount factor can be generalized as:

Discount factor = $(1/(1+\text{interest rate}))^{\text{years}}$.

ACTIVITY 7.4 CALCULATING THE DISCOUNT FACTOR

What would be the discount factor for income to be received in four years' time if the interest rate remains at 4 per cent?

We can now apply these calculations to the two proposals A and B. The cash flows for each year are multiplied by the relevant discount factors to obtain discounted cash flows (DCFs). These are totalled to get an overall figure for the proposal, as shown in Tables 7.3 and 7.4. We will assume the current interest rate is 5%.

TABLE 7.3 *DCFs for proposal A (in £s)*

Year	Out-goings	Income	Cash flow	Accumulated cash flows	Discount factor (5%)	DCF
0	10,000	0	−10,000	−10,000	1.0000	−10,000.00
1	4,000	2,000	−2,000	−12,000	0.9524	−1,904.76
2	1,000	3,000	2,000	−10,000	0.9070	1,814.06
3	1,000	8,000	7,000	−3,000	0.8638	6,046.86
4	1,000	10,000	9,000	6,000	0.8227	7,404.32
Totals	17,000	23,000	6,000			3,360.48

TABLE 7.4 *DCFs for proposal B (in £s)*

Year	Out-goings	Income	Cash flow	Accumulated cash flows	Discount factor (5%)	DCF
0	10,000	0	−10,000	−10,000	1.0000	−10,000.00
1	1,000	10,000	9,000	−1,000	0.9524	8,571.43
2	1,000	8,000	7,000	6,000	0.9070	6,349.21
3	1,000	3,000	2,000	8,000	0.8638	1,727.68
4	4,000	2,000	−2,000	6,000	0.8227	−1,645.40
Totals	17,000	23,000	6,000			5,002.92

The total DCF, to the nearest pound, for proposal A is £3,360 and for B it is £5,003. In general, if total DCF for a proposal is positive it means that the proposal would generate more money than if the investment were in a bank at the selected interest rate. If the figure is negative it means that the proposal would generate less money than leaving money on deposit at the selected interest rate.

ACTIVITY 7.5 RE-CALCULATING NPVS

Recalculate the NPVs for the two proposals assuming an interest rate of 8 per cent.

Stacey (1993), among others, has pointed out that the predicted flows needed for this method are very uncertain. Analysts who apply DCF analysis usually repeat the calculation with varying assumptions about, for example, the prevalent interest rate, costs and market share. They can then examine how these variations might affect the project outcome. We have already suggested the need for the consideration of a number of different scenarios. However, the downside is that where a wide range of scenarios with a large number of parameters is considered, this may confuse rather than clarify things. There is a temptation to select as the most likely scenario the one that gives the desired outcome and some objectivity may in fact be lost. As Stacey comments: '*in practice the use of what appear to be highly rational techniques may all too often simply be a cover-up for decisions being taken on other bases'* (Stacey 1993, p. 37).

Risk assessment

A recurring theme in this chapter is that plans are based on assumptions that are uncertain. In the last section, for example, we suggested that business plans be evaluated by looking at a number of different future scenarios. We are going now to take this idea further and assess specific risks inherent in a business proposal. Finding risks does not necessarily mean that the proposal is not adopted: we might be able to do things to avoid or reduce a risk that has been identified.

Trying to open a discussion about risk can sometimes be difficult. Proponents of a particular possibly money-making scheme can be super-enthusiastic and driven. As Mike Southon (author of *The Beermat Entrepreneur*) says:

> *'if you talk to entrepreneurs about failure they don't listen. They don't countenance the idea that their idea might not work. If it does end up failing, it is never down to them. It is down to some other factor....'*
>
> (Chadwick 2005)

Obviously, if the resources that are being invested are all your own, then you are entitled to take risks. Where the money is coming from other people, a more sober approach is needed.

This does not mean that large organizations are completely risk-averse. They are likely to have a number of business developments in progress at any one time. They are probably used to the idea that some developments may be more or less successful than others. The key questions will be the amount of risk involved in any particular proposal and the plans that are in place to deal with the most significant of those risks.

A major element of risk is uncertainty. Uncertainty often springs from a lack of knowledge and can be dispelled by investing in activities that buy knowledge. Thus risk reduction should be a driver during the whole proposal and planning phase. In particular, the research process, especially investigating the market, can be a powerful means of reducing lack of knowledge and thus risk. As the planning develops, further risks will appear and steps can be taken to ensure that the potential dangers are avoided.

> Recall the use of data mining to verify hypotheses that was discussed in Chapter 5.

However, despite this on-going process and all the care exercised by analysts and planners, some uncertainties and potential dangers will remain.

It is these residual risks that will be the concern of this section of the business proposal report.

Risks can broadly be divided into two types: **business risks** and **project risks**. IT practitioners, particularly those who have been involved with project management, are likely to be very familiar with project risk. For the project manager, the objectives of the project can be seen as:

- delivering the agreed functionality,
- on time,
- within budget,
- at the agreed level of quality.

Project risks are those things that can prevent these objectives being met.

Boehm (1991), for example, has identified a set of risks to projects that are to deliver software – see Table 7.5.

TABLE 7.5   *Barry Boehm's 'Top 10' software development risks (Boehm 1991)*

Risk	Risk reduction techniques
Personnel shortfalls	Staffing with top talent; job matching; teambuilding; training and career development; early scheduling of key personnel
Unrealistic time and cost estimates	Multiple estimation techniques; design to cost; incremental development; recording and analysis of past projects; standardization of methods
Developing the wrong software functions	Improved software evaluation; formal specification methods; user surveys; prototyping; early user manuals
Developing the wrong user interface	Prototyping; task analysis; user involvement
Gold plating	Requirements scrubbing; prototyping; cost-benefit analysis; design to cost
Late changes to requirements	Stringent change control procedures; high change threshold; incremental development (deferring changes)
Shortfalls in externally supplied components	Benchmarking; inspections; formal specifications; contractual agreements; quality assurance procedures and certification
Shortfalls in externally performed tasks	Quality assurance procedures; competitive design or prototyping; contract incentives
Real-time performance shortfalls	Simulation; benchmarking; prototyping; tuning; technical analysis
Development technically too difficult	Technical analysis; cost-benefit analysis; prototyping; staff training and development

A development project will therefore be seen as a success if the required deliverables have been created and the targets above have been hit. However, there are still risks of a seemingly well-crafted IT product or service not being a business success. It might not generate the expected cost savings, increased sales or other business objective originally set.

Project risks can be seen as a subset of business risk. If, for example, development costs exceed the original budget then this might mean that the new capability is no longer profitable.

Some IT project managers may shrug off the business risks that do not spring from the development project itself as not their concern as the IT project manager already has enough problems. However, given the key theme of ebusiness strategy is the fusion of business and IT concerns, this viewpoint becomes less justifiable.

In consultation with key stakeholders the business analyst must document the most significant perceived risks. Not all candidate risks can be managed, so some order of priority needs to be allocated. The classic way of doing this is to identify a risk exposure value calculated as:

Risk exposure = (cost of the damage) × (probability of occurrence).

Here is a very simplistic example. Say 10,000 orders a year were projected for a new product with a selling price of £100. It might be estimated that the proportion of non-payments, for example because of bad debts, was 3 per cent. This would give a risk exposure of (£100 × 10,000) × 3%, that is £30,000. This implies that £30,000 should be set aside in a pool to compensate for non-payments.

In this example it is easy for organizations to assess the risk because they will have past records in their accounting systems of the proportion of bad debts. However, the very nature of the development process means that we are usually dealing with novel circumstances where there are few previous examples to help us. This means that project managers will be unable to provide precise probabilities of possible risks.

In this case rather than use exact numeric values, the manager might be asked to rate the damage or impact and its probability using more qualitative descriptions such as 'high', 'significant', 'moderate' and 'low'. To avoid inconsistencies in the application of these ratings, they can be mapped onto ranges of values. An example of the mapping in the case of risks that might affect the impact on cost is given in Table 7.6.

TABLE 7.6 *Mapping risk descriptors to ranges*

Descriptor	Mapping
High	20% or more above the target cost plus error margin
Significant	Up to 20% above the target cost plus the error margin
Moderate	Greater than 50% of the error margin, but still within it
Low	Within 50% of the error margin

The problem with using qualitative descriptors is that there is no easy way of combining the impact and probability as there is where both are presented as numbers. As an alternative each risk can be plotted on a probability–impact grid – see Figure 7.2.

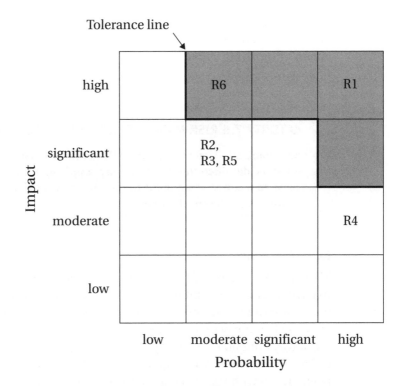

Tolerance line

FIGURE 7.2   *A probability–impact matrix*

The numbers of R1, R2 etc. refer to particular risks. The closer they are to the top right corner of the grid, the more seriously they should be taken. The tolerance line shows the area within which risks are seen as being particularly serious.

Having identified the project-threatening risks, the next question is what to do about them. This will depend on whether the costs of any actions to manage the risk are justified by the seriousness of the risk. In the previous example there was a 3 per cent risk of non-payment. A proposal might be made to introduce more rigorous credit checks which, it is estimated, could reduce the non-payment rate to 1 per cent. This would cut the risk exposure from £30,000 to £10,000, a saving of £20,000. If the new procedures cost £25,000 to operate, managers might decide that the risk reduction activity was not worth it.

Risk reduction activities focus on reducing the likelihood of the risk occurring. The cost of the risk reduction is incurred whether the potential danger materializes or not. **Risk mitigation** in the shape of a **contingency plan** comes into operation when what was a potentially damaging event has occurred. Its objective is to limit the damage as far as possible. In the example concerning bad debts, a debt-chasing regime might be instituted to deal with non-payments. In this case most costs are only incurred when the risk actually materializes, but often some upfront costs have to be met to enable the contingency actions. For example, the contingency action of restoring a database that has been corrupted requires back-ups to have been taken.

ACTIVITY 7.6 RISK MANAGEMENT AND OTS SOFTWARE

An organization decides to buy an OTS application to run its payroll. A risk is identified that the company supplying the software might cease to trade at some point in the future. What risk management actions might be considered?

Exit strategies

Many people find the idea of prenuptial agreements which set out who is to have what in the event of a divorce rather against the 'until death do us part' spirit of matrimony. Some people might feel the same about setting out an exit strategy to be carried out if a project has to be abandoned. It is not always possible to simply cut a development or operation dead in order to save any further expenditure. For example, contracts may have been placed with suppliers and customers that will need to be honoured. Costly physical infrastructure – imagine the problems of decommissioning a nuclear power station – may have been put in place.

The existence of a well-defined exit strategy will have the effect of reassuring potential investors that there are clearly marked limitations on the liabilities that they face if they accept the proposed project.

The management plan

This explains how the implementation is to be managed. The responsibilities will be allocated for the tasks identified in the outline implementation plan (see the section on the 'Outline implementation plan' above). Key decision points or **milestones**, where a health-check on the state of the implementation is taken, should be identified. Implementation may involve setting up a range of projects that are managed as a programme – see the section on 'Implementation through programme management'.

IMPLEMENTATION ISSUES

Delivery options

Here we look at some of the options available that could be considered when thinking about how a new software application could be created. The decisions made will be documented in the 'Outline implementation plan' section of the business proposal report.

More technically minded IT specialists may jump at the opportunity to develop new code in-house. However, because of the risks associated with novel software development, other options need to be considered first. These include:

- off-the-shelf (OTS) or 'shrink-wrapped' software;
- customized off-the-shelf (COTS) software;
- open source software;
- application service providers (ASPs).

Each of these will now be considered in turn.

Off-the-shelf software

This is sometimes called 'shrink-wrapped' software. Where the application is generic, for example a sales order processing system, then a ready-made application could be considered. The advantages of OTS purchases include the following.

- It is likely to be cheaper as the supplier is able to distribute the costs of development across a large number of customers.
- As the application already exists, we can examine the way that it works and sound out the views of existing users.
- As the application already exists we do not have to wait for it to be constructed.
- If the package is well-established and has a broad customer base, the reliability of the application is likely to be high as previous users will have effectively debugged the application for us. However, after installation, some testing will be needed in order to ensure that the system has been set up correctly.
- We should be able to depend on the supplier for upgrades when statutory changes are made and when faults are found in the software.

> As was seen in Chapter 6, this is often the case with ERP applications.

OTS applications do, however, have some drawbacks – see, for example, Fairley (1994). These include the following.

- Because they already exist, there may be mismatches between the way that the application works and the way that the organization does things. The business may end up changing the way that it does things in order to fit in with the constraints of the software. There could of course be additional, non-financial, reasons for taking a risk reduction action, such as, for example, compliance with audit requirements.
- Elsewhere we have discussed how the innovative use of IT applications can give an organization a competitive advantage over its rivals. An OTS application means that your competitors could have exactly the same software as you.

- The supplier will retain ownership of the code that makes up the application. If new requirements emerge, the supplier would need to be persuaded to implement these changes. They may decline to do so unless the need is shared by large proportion of their clients.
- There could be particular problems if the supplier were to cease to trade. The users of the application might not then have access to the source code and would not be in a position to implement statutory changes to the software. One way for this risk to be reduced is to make use of an escrow service where copies of the software are deposited with a third party who can release the code to its users in the event that the supplier ceases to trade – see Holt and Newton (2004) for further information about escrow.
- As an OTS application tends to be self-contained there may be problems in getting it to interoperate with other applications that the organization might have.

Although the acquisition of OTS software requires significantly less effort than in-house software development, the amount of work and management involvement needed should not be underestimated. Detailed requirements gathering and a rigorous selection process would need to be followed. Complex, widely used, applications such as those supplied by SAP rely on the appropriate selection of large sets of parameters in order to meet the individual requirements of each client. This can be a time-consuming process. As noted earlier, there may be discrepancies between the demands of the new application and the way the organization has previously done business and considerable training may be needed to deal with this.

Customized off-the-shelf applications

There is some confusion about the acronym COTS. Here we are using the term for situations where a supplier has a core set of code for an application domain and modifies it to produce a variant for an individual client. One example of this was where a standard commercial invoicing system was modified to deal with the collection of student fees. Sometimes, however, COTS is said to stand for *'commercial off-the-shelf'* and is used to refer to the type of shrink-wrapped applications that were the subject of the previous section. However, throughout this book we have used COTS to refer to customized OTS.

A COTS solution is likely to be more expensive than a standard OTS solution, but there will be less chance of discrepancies between the resulting functionality and the way an organization works.

The additional work may be able to introduce features that are unique to the organization and which could give it a competitive advantage over its rivals. It is normally the case that intellectual property rights over the code will be retained by the developers, and they could sell the version with the new features to other customers unless there were terms in the contract guaranteeing the customer exclusive use of the new functionality.

There would also be questions about maintenance and upgrades of the code. The supplier will generally be very reluctant indeed to give the client access to the source code. This means that the client would need to return to the supplier if they wanted the system upgraded. Needless to say, this puts the supplier in a very strong bargaining position over the pricing of additional work.

Open source

It is difficult to think of many businesses that only use software that they themselves have written. For a start why develop the operating systems and desktop utilities that are common to all IT sites? The nature of the software used to communicate with external organizations and individuals means that it has to use common code developed by a third party. It clearly makes sense to use well-established and commonly used software for these fundamental processes.

However, it can also be seen that licensing this crucial software from third parties also carries serious risks. For example, what if the supplier brings out a new version of the software for which it charges exorbitant licence fees and then refuses to support old versions?

This threat has made open source software a very attractive option. Open source software can usually be acquired for no charge apart from the fees to cover the cost of the transfer. The software is developed by volunteers who work on the application for no direct financial award. Anyone can have access to the source code and can make their own amendments. There is a controlling individual or body which can evaluate amendments and incorporate changes that add value to the software.

Examples of open source software include the Linux operating system, the OpenOffice office suite, MySQL database management software and Apache web service software. It also includes Sendmail, email transfer and management software that in 2004 was used by about 80 per cent of the world's mail servers and BIND, the major addressing system used by the internet (Weber 2004).

Open source software is enabled by the existence of a special type of open source license. The details of these can vary, but there are three distinctive features:

- the source code must be distributed with the software or otherwise be made available for no more than the cost of distribution;
- anyone who receives the software may distribute it to others free of charge and without having to provide royalties or licensing fees to the original authors;

- anyone can modify the code and then distribute the modified code under the same terms as the original license (Open Source Initiative 2002).

A clear initial advantage of open source software is, of course, that it is free, that the software can be acquired free of charge. This does not mean that there is no cost. The loose affiliation of developers that have created the software will not be available to install it for you or to offer the kind of support that commercial suppliers of software can offer. Luckily, there are now firms, Red Hat being one of the most well-known, who will install the software and provide support for the 'free software' on a payment basis.

You might think that IT managers would be cautious about the likely quality of software that has been produced by volunteers without payment. In fact many open source applications have a better reputation for reliability than the offerings of major commercial software suppliers. Partly this is because mature open source products have a huge number of users who effectively carry out massive field trials and an army of unpaid maintenance staff who debug faults as they emerge. An adage of open source is that *'with enough eyes all bugs are shallow'*.

Theorists and researchers in the fields of economics and political science have been fascinated by the open source phenomenon – see, for example, Steven Weber (2004). On the face of it, it runs against the received wisdom of the need for economic reward to motivate development. There is not space here to discuss the motivations that have been suggested. However, one motivation for an organization applies if there is no particular competitive advantage in preventing other people using your software. By making the software open source, you can move the burden of on-going mainte-nance and enhancement to the user community as a whole.

Application service providers (ASPs)

The discussion of shrink-wrapped and COTS solutions above has assumed that the application would run on a hardware platform within the purchaser's organization. When the software solution is selected, this could require the purchase of a compatible hardware configuration. An alternative would be to employ the services of an ASP. An ASP provides access to a software application that does not reside on the customer's IT hardware platform but is hosted by the supplier. The general concept is as old as the use of computers in business. In the early days of computing, hardware costs were astronomical and all but the largest corporations were likely to buy time from 'computer bureaux' to run applications like payroll. The advent of the web which allows the flexible delivery of services via the internet has reinvigorated the idea.

ASPs often provide access to software applications developed by third parties. The major financial benefit for users is that charging is normally based on a monthly per-user fee. Thus heavy initial set-up costs may be avoided. The monthly charges may mean that expenditure on the application is easier to budget at the outset than the expenses associated with in-house provision. Out-goings using this approach count as current expenditure rather than capital. Over the longer term, however, renting is usually more expensive than buying.

> ## ACTIVITY 7.7 THE EFFECT OF ASP SOLUTIONS ON CASH FLOWS
>
> **In general terms how would the pattern of cash flows that come from using an ASP solution affect the financial indicators of the business feasibility of a project described in the section on the 'Financial case'?**

From the broader business point of view the benefits usually claimed for outsourcing can be cited here. For example, it is argued that the use of an ASP means that the client organization can focus on the key areas where they are able to add business value and not be distracted by issues relating to IT provision.

The use of ASPs can be seen as an intermediate form of outsourcing. The access to an IT system might be just one part of a broader set of services supplied externally. For example, Amazon is reported as being about to supply warehousing facilities to other businesses.

IMPLEMENTATION THROUGH PROGRAMME MANAGEMENT

The motivation for programme management

The material here is based loosely on the programme management approach advocated by the OGC in the publication *Managing Successful Programmes* (Office of Government Commerce 2003). Our concern here is that the reader obtains an understanding of the ideas and principles of the approach. For a fuller grasp of the finer details the interested reader is directed to the appropriate OGC publications.

It will be recalled that because of the range of different types of specialist expertise needed to implement an ebusiness proposal, it is often better to manage the implementation as a **programme**. In this context we are using the term 'managed programme' to describe a co-ordinated set of projects that together contribute to a common set of outcomes.

The programme management approach can be seen in some ways as a scaled-up version of the incremental project delivery model. The idea of increments, as originally popularized by Tom Gilb (1988), is to break development into small 'mini-projects', each of which delivers some benefits to the business. For ebusiness developments, this may be particularly useful as it means that some income may be delivered at an early stage which may reduce the overall debt incurred by the development.

151

> This idea has been taken up by the Atern/Dynamic Systems Development Method (DSDM) – see Stapleton (2002) and www.dsdm.org.

A key practice in the incremental approach is that of **time-boxing**. For each increment the delivery date is sacrosanct. The aim will be to deliver those products that will provide most benefit to the customer, while deferring the less useful elements. Although we have suggested an analogy between increments and the projects in a programme, programme management is not simply a scaled up form of project management as we will see in the next section.

Planning the programme

The setting up of a programme will be helped by the formulation of documents which correspond in the OGC approach to the **programme brief**, the **vision statement** and the **blueprint**. Each of these will be described in a little more detail below.

A **programme brief** is the equivalent of a feasibility study for the programme. It is likely to have sections which reflect those described above for a business proposal but will be at a higher level. A key element of it, however, will be a **vision statement**. This describes the new capability that the organization is to acquire through the programme. The capability might, for example, be the use of the internet as a new channel for conducting business for an established chain of department stores. The focus of the vision statement is very much on establishing the benefits of the desired destination.

A new capability such as the creation of an internet channel for conducting sales can only come about through changes to structure and processes in the organization. The **blueprint** will describe the required changes in terms of the new business models and workflows needed, any restructuring of the organization and supporting information systems. The expenditure, performance levels and agreed service levels needed to achieve the state of affairs described in the blueprint also need to be assessed and documented.

A commonly perceived failing of IT-based developments in the past has been the lack of obvious business benefits in terms, for example, of improved productivity. To counter this, the blueprint should be complemented by **benefit profiles** which record when the expected benefits from the capability will appear. In the case of the department store chain that is developing an internet channel for online sales, these would among other things predict the time when sales will start to be made through the new channel and how it is hoped these should grow as the new facility is publicized and promoted.

A value of documentation is as an aid to important business decision-making. An example is the **programme portfolio** which outlines the projects needed to fulfil the programme's objectives. This will set out the sequence and timing of these projects.

A **stakeholder map** may be helpful in identifying which groups have an interest in which parts of the programme. This is a preliminary step in creating a communications plan that explains how information is to be exchanged between the wide range of people who might be involved in the implementation.

Programme organization

Each project will have its own management structure, but the programme as a whole will also require an over-arching controlling function to co-ordinate the different activities that contribute to the outcomes of the programme. Figure 7.3 shows the structure for this that is recommended by the OGC approach. The top half of the structure labelled 'programme management' is the part that we want to look at here.

Programme management organization

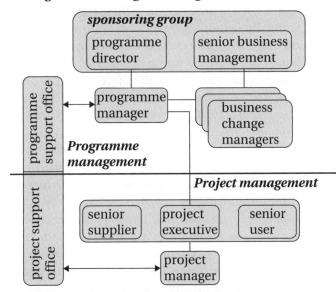

FIGURE 7.3 *Programme management organization*

The **programme director** is the 'political' head of the programme. He or she should be a senior person in the business with enough authority to ensure that the programme will be executed with energy. Such people are likely to be at a very senior level in the business (preferably at board level) and will have a range of responsibilities outside the programme. This means that the role of the programme director is often part-time.

The actual day-to-day oversight of the programme will be the full-time responsibility of the **programme manager**. This person ought to have extensive project management experience. The programme manager should also be familiar with the business needs of the organization. There is a risk that the programme manager may be distant from the practical operational aspects of the business. Partly this may be because programme managers often have a business analyst or IT background, but also because of their position outside the daily operation of the business. Thus **business change managers** who come from the operational areas are needed to provide guidance about operational issues. The business change managers are also responsible for co-ordinating the tasks that need to be carried out by operational staff.

Collecting progress information from and co-ordinating a number of projects within a programme can be time-consuming. These processes are likely to involve a large element of routine clerical processing and so a **programme support office** may be set up to collect progress information and analyse and distribute management information concerning individual projects within the programme.

Benefits management

A drawback of projects where there is no higher-level programme structure is that by definition the project team will be disbanded and dispersed at the end of the project. This means that the project manager will not be on hand during the operation of the capability that he or she helped to create. The project manager is therefore not in a position to ensure that the expected benefits that motivated the inception of the project in the first place have actually been experienced. Having a programme management structure that lives beyond the lives of individual projects means that there are people who can monitor the actual capture of the benefits. The programme manager, along with the business change managers, can take action to make sure that the benefits are actually achieved.

Business change managers will have a key role in ensuring that the new capabilities are exercised in a way that generates the expected benefits. For example, we had the case of the department store chain that wants to create an internet channel to supplement store sales. When the new channel is promoted, there may be a surge of interest as people want to try out the new way of buying things from an established brand. It could be that demand exceeds expectation for a short while leading to the part of the operation that deals with picking and dispatching being under pressure. This means that delivery times are extended. The dispatchers are aware that they are extremely busy, but may not be aware that delivery times are strategically important at this point as customers are less likely to become repeat visitors if delivery time is disappointing. A business change manager would be aware of the importance of delivery times, especially with a new website, and could institute urgent remedial measures such as employing additional, temporary, staff to deal with the unexpected peak in demand.

SELF-TEST QUESTIONS

1. Which of the following statements is TRUE?

   (a) A strategy is a master plan where every future move is thought through and planned in detail.

   (b) A strategy emerges through the interaction of a range of people within the organization with differing requirements.

   (c) Strategic management is piecemeal and has no defined view of the destination of the business.

   (d) The departure point for defining strategy is the current IT infrastructure and business practices.

2. A new computer-based system analyses data recorded by a particular type of scanning equipment used in the diagnosis of a medical complaint. One of the benefits of the new system would be improved diagnosis. This benefit of the system would be which of the following?

   (a) Quantified and valued.

   (b) Quantified but not valued.

   (c) Identified but not quantified.

   (d) Valued but not quantified.

3. A project's initial implementation cost is £18,000. The resulting application costs £1,000 a year for maintenance and support but saves £7,000 a year in staff costs. How long would be the pay-back period?

   (a) 3 years.

   (b) 2.57 years.

   (c) 2.14 years.

   (d) 2 years.

4. What is the current NPV of £100 that is to be received in three years time if the interest rate is 5 per cent?

   (a) £95.24.

   (b) £115.76.

   (c) £85.00.

   (d) £86.38.

5. Which of the following most accurately describes risk exposure?

   (a) The cost of damage caused if a risk actually materializes.

   (b) The probability that a risk will occur given the frequency of occurrences in the past.

   (c) The cost of damage if the risk occurs multiplied by the probability of it occurring.

   (d) A measurement of the degree to which damage inflicted by a risk if it occurred would be suffered by an individual stakeholder, calculated as a percentage.

Activity Pointers

CHAPTER 1 THE INTERNET, THE WEB AND BUSINESS OPPORTUNITY

Activity 1.1 The nature of networks

We make it six different paths:
1–2–4–5
1–2–4–3–5
1–4–5
1–4–3–5
1–3–4–5
1–3–5
Router 5 which is attached to C, would be isolated if 4–5 and 3–5 were cut. In this case, all the remaining routers would still be able to communicate with each other.

Activity 1.2 Establishing standards

When a barcode scanner made by a manufacturer is used by a retailer to read a product barcode that has been placed on the product by a supplier we can see that at least three stakeholders are involved.

There will need to be standards that ensure that manufacturers create barcode scanners that can accurately read the barcodes placed on products by suppliers and retailers. These standards will ensure that the barcodes put on products conform to certain physical characteristics such as size and definition.

There will need to be protocols about how barcodes are allocated to products so that each barcode is unique. As the suppliers of a product may supply the same product to a number of different retailers, they will not be enthusiastic about having a different barcode number for the same product for different customers. The need to allocate unique numbers implies the need for some central body to oversee the assignment of barcodes. An interesting parallel between the allocation of URLs and product barcodes is the hierarchical distribution of responsibility for allocating elements of a code. The product barcode had a prefix which identifies a company. The company can then add independently their own suffixes to identify uniquely particular products for which they are responsible.

Although individual codes do not have to be assigned centrally, to get full value from the system the codes, once assigned, need to be recorded in some central database.

For further information on barcodes look at the following websites: www.gs1uk.org and www.uc.council.org.

Activity 1.3 Limitations, constraints and disadvantages of the web

There could be lots of debate here. A list of some possible disadvantages of the web is presented below.

- **Information overload.** The web can provide too much detailed information. A simple example of this is when a search engine is used to access information on a topic and the researcher is overwhelmed with thousands of possible sources.
- **Information quality.** Anyone can place material on the web, so that the quality of the information provided can vary hugely, down to the deliberately misleading.
- **Security.** Because the web is all-pervasive and open, it is vulnerable to criminal and malicious operators.
- **Jurisdiction.** Because internet and web communications can so easily cross national borders, there may be problems in identifying who should be responsible for 'policing' the web. 'Policing' in some regimes might include trying to silence dissenting political voices, so there are very sensitive political issues involved in trying to gain international consensus.
- **Ephemerality.** Ebusiness websites do not necessarily have a 'bricks and mortar' equivalent which means that traders can come and go. A more mundane problem is that URLs can quickly become out of date – a particular problem when URLs are quoted in less transitory media like print.
- **Distrust.** The problems identified above could lead to people distrusting the web and thus be a constraint on ebusiness.

Activity 1.4 Sales that do not involve physical delivery

There are lots of possible examples including:

- insurance where the result of the contract would be an insurance policy, that is, an obligation to pay the customer an amount of money in the event of a specified type of future loss;
- placing a bet with an online bookmaker;
- where the supplier provides a service involving the customer going to the premises of the supplier, as in the case of cinemas, theatres, restaurants and so on.

Activity 1.5 Identifying revenue streams

www.tesco.com
This site has a wide range of revenue streams, including:

- selling insurance;
- processing digital photographs;
- downloading music;

- selling and delivering a very wide range of products;
- home delivery of groceries that have been ordered online.

This may seem to have a straightforward sales revenue model, but in some cases the products and services (in the case of financial products for example) are likely to be supplied by third parties, and thus the commission model would apply. Tesco also uses the website to seek for 'associates' who would be willing to put through links to the Tesco website in return for a percentage of the final sales value, or in the case of groceries an amount per referral. These click-throughs are facilitated by a special enabling company TradeDoubler.

www.ikea.co.uk

In contrast to Tesco, Ikea is very oriented to bricks and mortar. Ikea (at least in the UK) does not do home deliveries. The website might generate some interest by acting as an online catalogue, but the customer would still need to visit an Ikea outlet in order to purchase an actual product.

www.guardian.co.uk

The Guardian newspaper website includes the following revenue streams:

- advertising;
- mobile phone alert service;
- information about placing advertisements in The Guardian;
- various customer offers, including books and airline tickets, many of which must be serviced by third parties;
- selling subscriptions to full newspaper content.

An interesting question in the case of The Guardian and in the case of Tesco home delivery is that of the extent of **cannabalization**. This is where a web-based service, rather than generating new custom, is simply transferring existing customers to an online service from a more conventional means of exchange.

Self-test questions

1. (b)
2. (b)
3. (c)
4. (d)

CHAPTER 2 USING THE INTERNET TO GENERATE COMPETITIVE ADVANTAGE

Activity 2.1 Calculating net profits

(a) Net profit   = $(600 \times (£400 - £250)) - £50,000$

   = $£90,000 - £50,000$

   = $£40,000$

$$\text{Net profit per sale} \quad = \quad £40,000/600$$
$$= \quad £66.67$$

(b) Net profit $\quad = \quad (1200 \times (£400 - £300)) - £50,000$
$$= \quad £120,000 - £50,000$$
$$= \quad £70,000$$

Net profit per sale $\quad = \quad £70,000/1200$
$$= \quad £58.33$$

(c) Net profit $\quad = \quad (600 \times (£500 - £300)) - £50,000$
$$= \quad £120,000 - £50,000$$
$$= \quad £70,000$$

Net profit per sale $\quad = \quad £70,000/600$
$$= \quad £116.67$$

Activity 2.2 Generating customer value

These are some of the ways that a restaurant might try to generate customer value:

- quality of the food: using the best ingredients, methods etc.;
- wide variety of dishes;
- specialities or niches, for example vegan cuisine;
- quality of wines;
- service;
- location, for example with a nice view of the sea;
- décor or ambience – could have a theme;
- entertainment, for example live music;
- prestige;
- child friendliness.

Note that some of these features might appeal to some customer segments but not others.

Activity 2.3 Product differentiation

(a) **Personal computers.** The basic features and design of personal computers are fairly standard, although there may be differences in performance and advanced features.

(b) **Payroll software packages.** Payroll applications will tend to have the same functionality although there might be differences in such things as the type of management information available and the interfaces with other applications. There may be significant switching costs because differences in database structures might make it difficult to migrate data.

(c) **Printer cartridges.** There are differences between the types of cartridge used by different makes of printer.

(d) **Computer stationery.** Basic stationery, for example A4 plain, is an undifferentiated commodity product; however, specialized stationery might be produced for specific organizations, for example for payment cheques.

(e) **Computer games.** The most differentiated of these products – although there might be some similarities between some games, the market thrives by bringing in a constant flow of new and original products.

Activity 2.4 Five forces analysis

Factor	Impact	Rating
Large proportion of sales go to a relatively small number of buyers	Brightmouth PC is in a better position than a single domestic purchaser, but is still quite small – however, see the note on the special position of retailers	Low/medium
Purchase is a high proportion of the buyers' costs	This is very much the case with Brightmouth PC. Buyers could be very motivated to look at alternative sources of PCs if prices seem high	High
Product is undifferentiated	Standardization of PCs and their operating systems means that it is relatively relatively easy to switch to another make	High
Low switching costs	See above	High
Low profits for buyers	Given that Brightmouth PC work in a very competitive market it is likely that price competition keeps profits low	Medium/ high
Buyers pose a credible threat to backward integration	There is a probability that retailers could assemble the various components of a workstation from different sources	Medium
The industry's product is unimportant to the quality of the buyer's products and services	If Brightmouth PC is focusing on the business market then the performance and reliability of the PCs may be a concern and they may be willing to pay more for performance and reliability	Low
Buyer has full information	It might be easier for a wholesaler to keep the prices they charge to retailers confidential	Medium

Note that retailers can exert power over their suppliers if they are able to influence end-purchasers over their choice of product through their recommendations and advice.

Activity 2.5 The value of start-up companies

One reason is that investors thought that a business was not currently making a profit because it was focusing on gaining a commanding share of the market. It would then be able to make considerable profits later. Given that competition tends to increase with maturity, this has considerable risks.

Self-test questions

1. (d)
2. (b)
3. (b)
4. (a)
5. (a)

CHAPTER 3 THE VALUE CHAIN AND THE INTERNET

Activity 3.1 Adding value

(a) For suppliers, the uses of RFID tags described would be part of outward logistics, but for the purchaser they would be inward logistics. This is typical of IT-based supply chain applications that span organizations.

(b) This would probably be seen as part of human resources management.

(c) There could be some argument over this. As the customer is effectively on the way to delivering the goods to their own house, this seems to be outward logistics. The POS equipment also would be capturing valuable information to support marketing and sales.

(d) A case could be argued here for either outward logistics or sales and marketing. Our view tends towards sales and marketing as these activities include pricing in order to maximize sales and profits.

(e) Acquiring office materials such as stationery is a procurement activity. It is not inward logistics because stationery is not incorporated into the products that are sold.

Activity 3.2 Applying the value chain model to a bank

As is seen later in the chapter, Charles Stabell and Øysteb Fjeldstad had problems with applying the value chain model to banks. The diagram below illustrates our approach to the problem.

Our rationale for this model is that the financial benefits a customer of the bank receives are those things listed under outward logistics, i.e. getting a loan, getting interest on deposits and taking money out of the account.

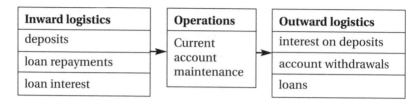

Inward logistics	Operations	Outward logistics
deposits	Current account maintenance	interest on deposits
loan repayments		account withdrawals
loan interest		loans

We would argue that opening an account and making deposits are not in themselves customer benefits – they allow the benefits listed under 'outward logistics' to be experienced. As will be seen in the main text, Stabell and Fjeldstad argue that the essential service a bank provides is bringing together people with spare money who can profitably put it out to loan with people who need to borrow money. Thus, it is argued, a different model from the value chain is needed – the value network.

Activity 3.3 Value chains, shops and networks

Once again there is often no clear-cut answer.

(a) In some ways, an insurance broker could be seen as a value shop. A customer could come for advice on an insurance matter. This could be regarded as a problem to which a solution in the form of a particular type of insurance policy is offered. An alternative view could be that the insurance brokers are providing a value network bringing potential customers for insurance together with suitable insurers.

(b) This may seem like a value network, but the car dealer has already bought the cars that are on sale, so the more traditional value chain model may be more appropriate.

(c) If the club is for amateurs, it seems to us that this is definitely a value network, bringing together people who want to play football into teams and then arranging matches with other teams.

(d) If the rock star generates income by selling CDs and downloads, then this seems to be a value chain. Performances could also be seen as a service that is the delivery point of a value chain.

Activity 3.4 Disaggregating the activities of a university

Firstly, we would like to make it clear that we do **not** think that a university is – strictly speaking – a business. For a start it is not profit-making and it has some responsibilities to the community as a whole – such as contributing to the creation of people with needed professional skills – not just to students as 'customers'. Clearly there could be lots of argument about this.

An incomplete list of value-generating units includes:

- teaching;
- assessment – many organizations set and mark examinations but are not involved with teaching;
- contracted research of various types;
- consultancy;
- publications;
- conferences;
- hiring out of premises;
- accommodation (e.g. halls of residence);
- catering;
- library services;
- computer services;
- careers advice;
- industrial placements.

Some examples of external organizations as competitors or outsourcers include:

- teaching: university courses being taught at 'franchised' institutions, for example further education colleges in the UK and private colleges abroad, can be seen as outsourcing;
- assessment: universities can prepare students for examinations of other bodies such as professional bodies, which is outsourcing;
- accommodation: there is usually some 'competition' with halls of residence from private providers of accommodation such as landlords renting out houses; the management of halls of residence could be outsourced;
- catering: once again catering in refectories etc. could be outsourced.

Intriguing possibilities could be to spin-off library services, perhaps to a local authority, and careers advice and industrial placements to a recruitment agency.

The area of core university activities is in fact very controversial. It might seem that teaching and assessment are core activities, but as we saw above both of these can in effect be outsourced. On the other hand, some argue that a university is about a complete experience for the undergraduates, with communal living as part of this experience, so accommodation and catering are thus core activities.

Activity 3.5 Making a purchase

There is clearly no one correct answer to this. Likely general approaches are discussed in the main text.

Activity 3.6 Inward delivery strategy

Potentially there is a conflict between getting a discount for a bulk order and having frequent deliveries of small numbers of units. For the arrangement of having a large number of small deliveries to work, the supplier must know that the customer is committed to further orders over time. Sometimes a contract is negotiated where the customer agrees to take a fixed number of units over a period of time, but can 'call off' instalments of deliveries as required during that period.

Self-test questions

1. (b)
2. (b)
3. (a)
4. (d)
5. (d)

CHAPTER 4 THE BUSINESS AND TECHNOLOGICAL ENVIRONMENT

Activity 4.1 SWOT analysis

Note: this is an example of the possible outcome of a brain-storming session. It does not pretend to be definitive, but is designed simply to generate some discussion points.

Mobile phones	PC-based email
Strengths	
• Handsets are relatively cheap	• Emails are very cheap, sometimes free
• Pay-as-you-go is a simple payment method	• Recipient of a message does not have to be available at time of delivery in order to receive message
• Voice-based – minimal dexterity needed in basic mode	• Permanent record of communication
• Conversations are very interactive	• Cheap overseas communication
• Newcomers to the technology probably already use telephones – a familiar technology	• Facilities to open communication to further parties by forwarding, 'carbon copies' etc.
• Easy to carry around	• Large display
• Can be used discreetly	• Typewriter QWERTY keyboard is familiar to many
Weaknesses	
• Geographical coverage can be patchy	• Needs relatively expensive PC/laptop
• Infrastructure of masts needed	• Not all people have internet access – telephone coverage is greater
• Can be expensive	• Unsolicited emails (Spam)
• Overseas calls can be very expensive	• Danger of viruses
• Not very secure	• Danger of phishing
• Text input is possible but is slow	• Needs access to telephone landline

(Continued)

(Continued)

Mobile phones	PC-based email
Weaknesses	
• Display is limited	• Location tends to be fixed because of size of workstation and need for internet access
• Battery life is a limitation	
• Use in public places can be seen as anti-social	
Opportunities	
• Convergence with email/internet	• Voice over IP: cheap voice phone calls
• 3G developments, e.g. possibility of watching videos	• Wireless connections, WiMax etc. increases mobility
• Downloading music	• Getting smaller, e.g. palm-tops
• Camera	• Instant messaging
Threats	
• Saturation of the market	• Specialist devices could undermine the general purpose PC
• Malicious hacking could spread to mobile systems	• Improved mobile phone technology and features
• Increase in complexity of interface	
• VOIP as an alternative	

It can be argued that technological developments are tending to lead to a convergence of the two types of device and that in future one single device would have both functions. A counter-argument is that separate types of device are likely to survive as there are distinct uses for the devices. Mobile phones are portable, personal devices, used mainly to communicate with friends and family – use tends to be informal. While email can, of course, be used informally, PCs tend to be used in more formal settings, for example in offices. Some of the features of PC-based email are ideal for work environments, for example having the potential to keep a permanent record of communications.

Activity 4.2 A lifts database: environmental scanning

Sociocultural

Among the factors that would need to be considered would be:

- willingness of people to offer lifts;
- willingness of people to accept lifts;
- awareness of environmental issues;
- feeling of community – people are more likely to share lifts with people they know or with whom they can identify, for example those from the same community;

- geographical distribution of lift providers and lift users – if all the providers live in one place and all the users in another then there is likely to be an imbalance between supply and demand.

Economic

The cost of travel by public and private means could have an impact on the attractiveness of the scheme.

An issue here is the motivation for a car-sharing scheme. If the main motivation is environmental, then the aim would be to convert non-sharing motorists into car-sharers. Converting current public transport users into lift-sharers would give the impression that the car-sharing scheme is successful in terms of numbers, but would not have an impact on the environment. If a motivation was also to provide a means of cheaper travel, then recruiting public transport users would be seen as an indication of success.

Many car-sharing schemes are sponsored by employing organizations. For these organizations car-sharing may have a financial benefit as fewer car-parking spaces would be needed. It may even be worthwhile for such organizations to provide financial inducements to employees to car-share.

Political

The central government has a declared policy of supporting car-sharing. There are Department for Travel publications (e.g. Department for Transport 2004) that offer advice on car-sharing schemes.

Local government authorities also often support such schemes. Traffic systems may be modified to encourage car-sharing schemes by the introduction of HOV (High Occupancy Vehicle) lanes. A condition of approving planning permission for a new building might be that car-sharing schemes be introduced.

Legal

As noted later in the main text, the impact on the driver's tax and insurance position if lifts are offered needs to be explored and publicized. There may in fact be no problems here, but prospective car-sharers may need to be reassured if they are to join the scheme.

The ubiquitous Data Protection Act 1998 will need to be carefully considered as personal details, including home addresses, may be recorded on the system.

Ethical

Note that we have decided to deal with environmental issues as a specific type of ethical issue.

It has already been noted that if the scheme is designed to reduce the environmental impact of motor vehicles it should actually reduce rather than increase car use. If lots of people move from public transport, walking and cycling to car-sharing then car use might actually increase.

There are some risks to the safety of both drivers and passengers where these are unknown strangers. Some method of screening or identifying people might be considered. For example, they might have to be employees of the sponsoring organization. Interestingly a positive 'spin' can be put onto the security aspects of a car-sharing scheme by suggesting that they 'offer personal security benefits in the event of a breakdown, and the walk to and from car parks' (Department for Transport 2004).

Technological

Among the technical options that might be considered when implementing an IT-enabled system are:

- setting up a secure private group on a commercial car-sharing website;
- acquiring an OTS car-share software application;
- writing your own software system.

The use of GIS (geographical information system) components to support system could be considered.

Activity 4.3 Enablers and barriers to global reach

We have to be fair to Mr Hormats here as we do not know the precise context in which this statement was made – but this will not stop us from speculating. We think that the key point is that anything published on the web is immediately available across the globe. There is thus an immediate need for such material to be checked to be appropriate in all parts of the globe where it is accessed.

Where a business publishes material on the web, it is almost certainly to a greater or lesser extent going to have a promotional motivation. There is a risk that such material may inadvertently have a negative effect and repel prospective customers. Where a business is rooted in a particular locality and is only targeting local people then this risk is likely to be low. Where a company is a global brand, care must be taken to ensure the content of any website will be appropriate throughout the world. For example, it may not be possible to sell certain products in certain regions for legal reasons. Customers may react negatively if this is not made clear and they are subsequently disappointed.

As we will see, the web has not removed all barriers to international trade as there are constraints imposed by, for example, legal, financial and language differences.

Activity 4.4 Assessing barriers to adoption

	(a) Eprocurement in a local authority	(b) 'Self-service' updating of personal details	(c) COTS order processing system
Relative advantage	The cost saving advantages of eprocurement appear to be clear-cut and quantifiable	The advantages in terms of cutting human resources staff time are easily assessed. Advantages for employees while real may be less obvious	This depends on the degree to which the new system matches existing processes. The greater the gap, the more effort needed for implementation
Compatibility	Eprocurement requires some centralization as it needs a set of approved suppliers. However, this may not be as great as having bulk buying without IT support	This would be easiest to implement where staff have dedicated workstations. This is not the case with a supermarket	An OTS package is less likely to interoperate well with other systems in the organization. This might motivate a move to a complete ERP system covering all core organizational processes
Complexity	The ideas and benefits of eprocurement are simple to understand	The system is relatively easy to implement from an organizational point of view, but care is needed to win over employees	Order processing systems are generally well understood. Complexity may come from interfaces used to align the new system and existing practices and processes
Trialability	Eprocurement can be introduced on an incremental basis	The system can be implemented on an incremental basis.	The system is difficult to implement incrementally. A leap of faith may be required here
Observability	The benefits are easily measured financially and success stories are well-publicized as they reflect credit on both the authority and the supplier of the application	Benefits to the organization can be observed but these are not as clear-cut as in (a).	Benefits from COTS solutions are likely to be longer term and some time after the initial transition costs

Activity 4.5 Measuring attractiveness

We can all probably agree that the perception of 'attractiveness' varies from one individual to another. Even where there is a consensus that someone is attractive – say a film star – then this can be socially constructed. Tastes will vary in different societies and also over time.

For the purposes of measurement, the secret is to focus on the outcomes of a quality. In the case of software products, attractiveness is associated with the degree to which people will voluntarily use a software application. Measurements that might indicate the attractiveness of a software-based product include:

- the proportion of voluntary users who continue to use the software product after the initial introduction;
- the amount of time spent voluntarily using the software application.

Attractiveness is associated with use that is not mandatory. It could be argued that attractiveness may explain the continued use of software which has a low 'perceived usefulness' – people use the software for fun rather than to do anything useful.

Activity 4.6 Potential uses of mobile phones as an input device

(a) **Instructing a bank.** The main issue here would probably be the relative lack of security. For example, while the HSBC bank have enabled customers to use their mobile phones to obtain their current bank balance and to receive alerts when their monthly salary is paid in or they are going into the red, requesting payments is not yet implemented (Wray 2006a,b). Generally the use of mobile phones as a payment medium has been limited to relatively small transactions such as using texting to pay for ring-tones and the London congestion charge.

(b) **Railway season ticket renewal.** This may be less of a security problem than with the bank as payment method details could be set up beforehand, perhaps by a different medium, and would not have to be re-input. A new season ticket would need to be sent to you by post or you would need to pick it up. The need for a photograph might complicate things. The answer might be to use the same identify card with an automatic data input device at the railway station. Renewing the season ticket would then essentially update a database which would indicate that the card-holder continues to be a valid user.

   (Technologies are being developed where the mobile phone itself can be used as an input device in these kinds of circumstances. The Eden Project in Cornwall for example has a system whereby an image is downloaded onto the mobile phone which can be scanned by a device to enter the site.)

(c) **Traffic problem notification.** This would be an example of a **location-based service**. There could be road safety and legal issues here about using a mobile phone while driving unless a hands-free configuration can be guaranteed to be in place.

(d) **Software problem resolution.** The mobile phone could be used effectively as a pager. However, the amount and complexity of the text (which could include software code) seems to preclude the use of a mobile phone as an effective communication device to make bug fixes.

Activity 4.7 Potential uses of RFID and GPS

The characteristics of RFID systems use include:

- information is required to be held about specific physical objects, for example pallets of goods in warehouses, babies and surgery patients in hospitals, original paper documents in repositories;
- the location of the object may change and this needs to be tagged;
- the object originates or enters the system at a point where an RFID tag can be attached;
- the tagged object is at significant points of time in the proximity of a tag reader;
- as well as identification information, other data about the object may be incorporated in the tag, for example sell-by dates.

The GPS can be used to identify the location of an object anywhere in the world without it being close to a tag-reader. The GPS location information is transmitted to a receiver attached to the object itself, which can then transmit the information to other devices by other means. GPS locations tend to work with larger sized objects, for example a vehicle rather than a pallet.

Activity 4.8 Dealing with legacy systems

There is no single, at-a-stroke solution to this. However, strategies include the following.

Use of externally supplied OTS applications

For example, an ERP system which covers all the core generic commercial processes in an organization could be licensed from a supplier such as SAP. Because the same software is being used by a large number of organizations, there are economies of scale in such an arrangement as development costs are shared between many customers. The supplier should be able to afford to employ a larger number of more specialist staff to look after the application than a single user organization could. This approach, however, has some disadvantages:

- as everyone has the same system there is little opportunity to exploit the application to gain a competitive advantage;

- there is a danger of being locked into a particular supplier as it is difficult to change applications once they have been installed;
- there is a cost in customizing interfaces between the organization and the externally supplied IT system.

Outsourcing of software maintenance

The problems remain but are delegated to someone else. The maintenance could be carried out in a low-wage economy so costs are reduced.

Better structured software

A persistent theme over the past few decades is the need for well-structured software. Usually this focuses on software components having **high cohesion** and **low coupling**. High cohesion means that a component should, as far as possible, deal with a single externally apparent function and that as far as possible all the processing related to that function is - carried out within the component. Low coupling means that components are designed to reduce the need to communicate with other components to a minimum. The aspiration is that when a change is required, only one isolated component needs to be changed.

Re-factoring

A recognized problem with software is that over time, as changes accumulate, the code becomes more and more messy. Many approaches to software development stress the need for re-factoring code to keep it well-formed by rewriting components from scratch rather than tinkering with them as changes are required.

Self-test questions

1. (c)
2. (b)
3. (c)
4. (d)
5. (a)
6. (a)
7. (c)
8. (c)
9. (a)

CHAPTER 5 CUSTOMER RELATIONSHIP MANAGEMENT

Activity 5.1 Transactions versus relationships

(a) **Buying a newspaper.** On the face of it this seems like a simple transaction as the same newspaper could be bought from any of a number of different outlets. In terms of the newspaper itself, there is more of a relationship. I might identify strongly with a newspaper as it shares my general views on politics and society. There may be particular regular features I enjoy such as the crossword. Newspapers are very distinct brands. However, a newspaper may have very little in the way of information about individual readers.

(b) **Going to the dentist.** In the UK you would normally have to be registered with your dentist who hold your dental records. This seems to be very much like a relationship.

(c) **Buying a car.** This could be a one-off transaction. However, if the supplier of the car also provides maintenance services then this might contribute to the development of a relationship, particularly if there is a warranty period when the supplier is obliged to correct faults.

(d) **Booking a holiday abroad.** Once again this seems like a one-off transaction, unless perhaps you always go to the same hotel, for instance, because you know and like the staff.

Activity 5.2 Estimating losses through customer attrition

Year	Repeat business (a)	New business (b)	Total value of sales (£) (c)	Customers lost (d)	Carried forward (e)	Accum. number of lost customers (f)	Lost revenue (£) (g)
1	0	100	100,000	50	50	50	
2	50	100	150,000	60	90	110	50,000
3	90	100	190,000	68	122	178	110,000
					Total lost revenues		160,000

Below is an explanation of the table above.

(a) Repeat business. This refers to last year's customers who also book with the travel firm in the current year.

(b) New business. These are the new customers who have not booked up before.

(c) Total value of sales. This is the value of sales based on an average transaction value of £1,000. It is calculated as $((a)+(b)) \times 1,000$.

(d) Customers lost. This refers to current customers who do not come back in the following year. It is calculated as $((a) \times 0.2) + ((b) \times 0.5)$.

(e) Carried forward. These are the customers that do come back. It is calculated as $(a) + (b) - (d)$.

(f) Accumulated number of lost customers. These are all the customers who never came back. Note: we have not taken any account of customers who might miss a year and then come back to the travel company.

(g) Lost revenue. The value of sales lost through attrition in a particular year. It is based on the accumulated number of lost customers at the end of the preceding year.

Activity 5.3 Identifying global brands

When we did this as a training exercise, the Interbrand/Newsweek list was the most obvious source available (www.ourfishbowl.com/images/surveys/BGB06Report_072706.pdf accessed 15 April 2007). This had the following list:

1.	Coca-Cola	11.	Citi
2.	Microsoft	12.	Marlboro
3.	IBM	13.	Hewlett-Packard
4.	GE	14.	American Express
5.	Intel	15.	BMW
6.	Nokia	16.	Gillette
7.	Toyota	17.	Louis Vuitton
8.	Disney	18.	Cisco
9.	McDonalds	19.	Honda
10.	Mercedes	20.	Samsung

Some problems with using these lists are as follows.

- **The criteria for including and rating brands.** For example, the Interbrand/Newsweek list focuses on 'brand value' and assessment of the financial value that the brand adds to the basic product value. There may be different ways of calculating this and some aspects might need some estimation. The most well-known brands may not be the most valuable if they are for products which have a low individual unit price.
- **Regional brands.** Many very successful brands are regional rather than global.

Activity 5.4 Monetary decile analysis

Customer	Sales value	Decile	Total value	Percentage
f	252.50			
e	150.00	1st	402.50	46.02
b	100.00			
h	99.00	2nd	199.00	22.75
q	88.00			
m	43.00	3rd	131.00	14.98
c	25.00			
o	21.00	4th	46.00	5.26

(Continued)

(Continued)

Customer	Sales value	Decile	Total value	Percentage
a	20.00			
l	12.00	5th	32.00	3.66
j	11.50			
d	9.00	6th	20.50	2.34
s	6.60			
i	6.50	7th	13.10	1.50
g	6.00			
n	5.50	8th	11.50	1.31
t	5.50			
k	4.50	9th	10.00	1.14
p	4.50			
r	4.50	10th	9.00	1.03
	All sales		874.6	

Activity 5.5 Identifying a customer segment

The group was found to be students who called home regularly while they were at college. Although they had low incomes, most had access to parental support in the case of financial difficulties.

Self-test questions

1. (d)
2. (d)
3. (a)
4. (c)
5. (c)

CHAPTER 6 ENTERPRISE RESOURCE PLANNING SYSTEMS

Activity 6.1 Functions of a wholesale business

Among the many possible processes that have been omitted are the following.

Sales

A quotation might be requested by a potential customer before an order is placed. Goods might be returned by the customer as not fit for purpose. These might have to be returned to the original supplier. In some cases, refunds may have to be made.

Finance

Where customers do a lot of business, payments might not be made for each individual order and matching invoice. Instead, payments would be made when a monthly statement listing the invoices for the previous month is sent to the customer. Where a payment is due, but has not been received, a reminder would be sent. Another hazard is that a customer could pay by a cheque which is recorded, but it might be found that the cheque has 'bounced', that the customer does not have enough money in the bank to honour the cheque. In this case, the payment recorded would have to be cancelled by a bad cheque transaction.

Warehouse or inventory

There would need to be regular stock-takes to make sure the contents of the warehouse actually reflect what is recorded on the database. Where there are discrepancies, there would need to be transactions that adjust the stock levels recorded.

No doubt many other gaps can be found in the model.

Activity 6.2 Future repercussions of current events

A key point here is that additional information can help assess the impact of an event. It can also allow alternative courses of remedial action to be assessed more effectively.

(a) **Someone accepting a job offer.** An immediate consequence is that the business is committed to the expenditure needed to pay the new employee. There will be additional commitments when the person actually starts such as, for example, for office space, a workstation and access to corporate email and applications.

(b) **Receiving an order from a domestic consumer for a product.** This will trigger a delivery, which will reduce the level of stocks held. At some point stock will need to be replaced. Depending on the nature of the business this could trigger a production or a purchase process (or a mixture of both). The order will eventually be reflected in an increase in sales revenue.

(c) **An increase in the price of an important component of a popular product.** An increase in the price of a component would increase production costs. This would reduce profits. The business might seek to find an alternative supplier who might be able to supply the component at a lower price. In order to maintain profits, the business might decide to pass costs onto the customer. However, this might reduce sales if competitors are able to preserve lower prices.

(d) **An employee handing in their notice.** The work normally carried out by the departing member of staff will need to be re-planned. It might be possible, at least temporarily, to distribute work between remaining staff. A temporary benefit for the organization is that the staff budget will be reduced as the member of staff moves on. A recruitment process may be triggered if it is decided to fulfil the vacancy. The recruitment process itself will generate costs.

(e) **A unit of equipment used in a manufacturing process needing repair.** The probability is that it will not be possible to carry out one or more manufacturing processes. This would mean delays in making certain products. It may be that one or more specific orders were being satisfied by the production run that has been interrupted. The need to repair or replace the defective unit will affect the potential losses a business might experience.

Activity 6.3 Applicability of ERP systems

Given the brevity of the details provided, much of what follows can only be speculation.

(a) The growing proportion of effort being devoted to maintenance in both organizations suggests that the maintenance of legacy systems is swallowing up the IT development budget. If the two systems are to be merged then at least one of the organizations will have to change their way of working. It would appear that an ERP application might be a strong application for consideration, if one can be found that meets the particular needs of this sector.

(b) The question here is the degree to which it would be advantageous for the various constituent organizations to be integrated. There is also the need for variation to deal with local custom and practice. There would be an argument for some core financial accounting applications to be standardized which would allow consolidated financial information to be produced more easily.

(c) The accounting function seems to be largely outsourced already by the company. Considering the small size of the business and its specialist work the argument for ERP appears weak.

Activity 6.4 Package selection

The stages of a package selection process might include:

- analysis and documentation of requirements;
- drawing up an evaluation plan which indicates how the candidate packages might be compared and assessed;
- invitation to tender;
- evaluation of proposals – depending on the evaluation plan this might include:
  - scrutiny of proposal forms
  - interviewing suppliers' representatives
  - demonstrations
  - site visits
  - practical tests;
- vendor assessment;
- contract negotiation and placement.

Activity 6.5 ERP success factors

Project A

There is a large gap between the ERP reference model and the way the business works. It is difficult to change the ERP software, but not only is it relatively easy to change the business process, but the advantages of doing so can be identified. There are two primary influences that suggest not changing the software as opposed to only one that does (the large gap between the software and current procedures). It would appear that the option of changing the business processes would be favoured. This would increase the business benefits, but there would be some costs associated with changing the way the business operates.

Project B

The software is very easy to change, but there is already a close fit between business processes and the way the software works. In addition, it is easy to change the business processes, but not very desirable. Given that little or no change is needed for either the software or business processes, the project will probably be a success as efficiency gains are made by introducing IT, although basic procedures are not changed.

Activity 6.6 Reasons for *not* using web services

Execution of embedded code would be much faster than having to retrieve functionality across the web. Changes to external components could cause an application to malfunction. Such faults could be difficult to diagnose as those responsible for local applications would probably not have access to the internal workings of the web service.

Self-test questions

1. (b)
2. (d)
3. (d)
4. (a)
5. (a)

CHAPTER 7 FROM EBUSINESS STRATEGY TO IMPLEMENTATION

Activity 7.1 Draw up a conceptual model

Figure A.1 shows one possible conceptual model, which can be explained as follows.

1. **Identify work requirements.** The work to be carried out within the business will change with, among other things, developments in technologies and shifting market demands.

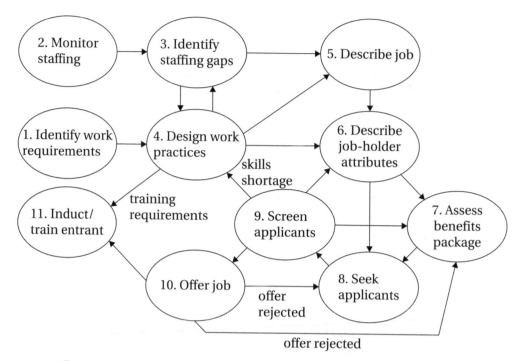

FIGURE A.1   *A possible conceptual map for part of a human resources system*

2.   **Monitor staffing.** Changes in staffing need to be monitored – for example, where a member of staff leaves, the possible need for a replacement would be identified.

3.   **Identify gaps.** A gap in staffing is identified. This could be triggered by a member of staff leaving or by new work practices being implemented.

4.   **Design work practices.** Changes in work requirements or staffing may lead to work practices being modified. For example, when someone leaves, working roles might be adjusted so that other people can cover the work of the departed colleague.

5.   **Describe job.** If a gap is identified that needs a new member of staff, a description of that job will need to be produced.

6.   **Describe job-holder attributes.** A profile of the kind of person to be recruited is produced. A judgement may need to be made about whether a person who is a very good fit for the job is to be sought or whether it is intended that training will be provided to overcome any shortfalls.

7.   **Assess benefits package.** Depending on the job-holder attributes a relevant salary range will be identified. In general, the more experience required, the higher the salary is likely to be.

8.   **Seek applicants.** For example, through placing advertisements.

9.   **Screen applicants.** This might lead to a job being offered to an applicant. A lack of suitable applicants might lead to the proposed salary being revised, the requirements of the job being reduced

('de-skilling') or less experienced applicants being targeted, but more training being planned.

10. **Offer job.** The offer may be accepted or rejected.
11. **Induct and train entrant.** The nature of the induction will depend on the work practices (which may involve new technology) and the experience of the new entrant.

Activity 7.2 Identifying financial benefits

(a) A key question here is the point when the customer makes their payment. If the payment is made on delivery, then the quicker the delivery the sooner the money will flow into the business. If, as with many ecommerce applications, payment is made with the order, it might actually be financially disadvantageous to incur the costs of supplying the order too quickly. Faster delivery, however, should lead to more repeat business through satisfied customers and more 'word of mouth' recommendations that could increase the volume of sales.

(b) The cost per transaction is reduced as the cost of creating, storing and delivering physical CDs is removed. The possibility of a 'stock-out' when a sale cannot be made as the supplier has run out of stock is also removed.

(c) The costs of running courses, for example payments to trainers, would be reduced. Unproductive travelling time where the training is off-site will be cut. As well as this saving, sales advisers may be able to use quiet periods to go through the training material, which will reduce the number of hours lost through training.

(d) This may improve the number of 'hits' for the associated website. An important factor will be the proportion of conversions of people who visit the website into customers who actually make a purchase. If the conversion rate ('book to look ratios') is maintained an increase in hits will follow through into an increase in sales.

Activity 7.3 Calculating the pay-back period

Year	Out-goings	Income	Cash flow	Accumulated cash flow
0	20,000	0	−20,000	−20,000
1	750	5,000	4,250	−15,750
2	750	5,500	4,750	−11,000
3	750	6,050	5,300	−5,700
4	750	6,655	5,905	205
		Pay-back	3.97 years	

Note that the pay-back period is calculated as 3 + absolute(−5,700)/5905, i.e. 3.97.

Activity 7.4 Calculating the discount factor

Year	Discount factor
1	0.9615
2	0.9246
3	0.8890
4	0.8548

The discount for the previous year is divided by 1 + (interest rate), in this case 1.04 for the 4 per cent interest rate.

Activity 7.5 Recalculating NPVs

If the interest rate was 8 per cent a year, then the NPVs would be as follows.

Proposal A

Year	Out-goings	Income	Cash flow	Discount factor	NPV
0	10,000	0	−10,000	1.0000	−10,000.00
1	4,000	2,000	−2,000	0.9259	−1,851.85
2	1,000	3,000	2,000	0.8573	1,714.68
3	1,000	8,000	7,000	0.7938	5,556.83
4	1,000	10,000	9,000	0.7350	6,615.27
Totals	17,000	23,000	6,000		2,034.92

Proposal B

Year	Out-goings	Income	Cash flow	Discount factor	NPV
0	10,000	0	−10,000	1.0000	−10,000.00
1	1,000	10,000	9,000	0.9259	8,333.33
2	1,000	8,000	7,000	0.8573	6,001.37
3	1,000	3,000	2,000	0.7938	1,587.66
4	4,000	2,000	−2,000	0.7350	−1,470.06
Totals	17,000	23,000	6,000		4,452.31

Note that NPV goes down as the interest rate goes up because it reflects the fact that I need less money now to get the same sum in the future. The NPV of proposal A is more affected as the higher interest rate is particularly damaging to proposed projects where the larger amounts of income come later in the project's life.

Activity 7.6 Risk management and OTS software

Many of the potential risk management actions are about to be discussed in the section on 'Implementation issues'. A risk avoidance action could be to write the payroll application in-house. ('Risk avoidance' is making a decision not to enter the situation or space where the risk exists – like not going into the sea so as to avoid sharks.) Risk reduction – reducing the chance of the risk occurring – could involve looking at the financial position of the supplier. It might be expected that the larger and more well-established the supplier and the larger the customer base, the lower the risk.

A risk mitigation action – one designed to reduce the damage if the risk materializes – could be to negotiate an escrow arrangement by which source copies of the software are deposited by the supplier with an independent entity which can release the software to the users if the supplier ceases to trade.

Activity 7.7 The effect of ASP solutions on cash flows

Here is a very simplistic example to illustrate the point. The introduction of a new software application will save £3,000 regardless of whether an outright purchase or an ASP solution is adopted. Rather than pay £10,000 outright, an annual fee of £2,500 is agreed. With this ASP solution there would still be some set-up costs which have been estimated at £1,000. Let us assume a 10 per cent interest rate to keep the arithmetic simple. Say the application would save the business £3,000 a year. The following tables show the situation.

Outright purchase option

Year	Out-goings	Income	Cash flow	Accumulated cash flow	Discount factors	DCF	Accumulated DCF
0	10,000	0	−10,000	−10,000	1.0000	−10,000.00	−10,000.00
1	0	3,000	3,000	−7,000	0.9090	2,727.27	−7,272.73
2	0	3,000	3,000	−4,000	0.8264	2,479.34	−4,793.39
3	0	3,000	3,000	−1,000	0.7513	2,253.94	−2,539.44
4	0	3,000	3,000	2,000	0.6830	2,049.04	−490.40
5	0	3,000	3,000	5,000	0.6209	1,862.76	1,372.36
6	0	3,000	3,000	8,000	0.5644	1,693.42	3,065.78
		Pay-back	3.5 years				

ASP solution

Year	Out-goings	Income	Cash flow	Accumulated cash flow	Discount factors	DCF	Accumulated DCF
0	1,000	0	−1,000	−1,000	1.0000	−1,000.00	−1,000.00
1	2,500	3,000	500	−500	0.9091	454.55	−545.45
2	2,500	3,000	500	0	0.8264	413.22	−132.23
3	2,500	3,000	500	500	0.7513	375.66	243.43
4	2,500	3,000	500	1,000	0.6830	341.51	584.93
5	2,500	3,000	500	1,500	0.6209	310.46	895.39
6	2,500	3,000	500	2,000	0.5645	282.24	1,177.63
	Pay-back	2 years					

These tables are similar to ones already shown in this chapter, except that we accumulate the DCFs. This shows what the outcome of the proposed course of action would be if the application was discontinued in a particular year.

It can be seen that the pay-back period is less for the ASP solution, as the initial costs are small and can be quickly paid off. If you look at the accumulated DCF figures for the two options it can be seen that if the ASP application was kept for four years the NPV would be better for that proposal. However, if the application was kept for five or six years then outright purchase would be better. Thus in general ASP solutions give better initial value, but as time goes on outright purchase gradually yields better value.

Self-test questions

1. (b)
2. (b)
3. (a)
4. (d)
5. (c)

Hughes, R. T., Al-Shehab, A. and Winstanley, G. (2006) Obstacles to the modelling of the causes of project success and failure. In Remenyi, D. (ed.), *Proceedings of the 5th European Conference on research methods in business and management.* MCIL, Reading, pp. 179–186.

Hughes, R., Cooper, A. and Marshall, T. (2002) What do the customers for IT products and services really want? *Proceedings of the UK Academy of Information Systems Conference,* Leeds Metropolitan University, 10–12 April.

Ibbott, C. J. and O'Keefe, R. M. (2004) Trust, Planning and benefits in a global inter-organizational system. *Inform. Syst. J.,* 14, 131–152.

ISO/IEE (2001) ISO/IEE 9126-1 Information technology: software product quality, Part 1. Quality model.

ISO/IEE (2003) ISO/IEE TR 9126-2003 Software engineering: product quality, Part 2. External metrics.

Johnson, G. and Scholes, K. (2002) *Exploring corporate strategy: text and cases,* 6th edition. Prentice-Hall, Harlow.

Jolly, A. (2006a) *A handbook of intellectual property management.* Kogan Page, London.

Jolly, A. (2006b) Hot property. *Computing Business,* April, pp. 34–35.

Kaplan, R. S. and Norton, D. P. (1992) The balanced scorecard – measures that drive performance. *Harv. Bus. Rev.,* 70(1), 71–79.

Keller, G. and Teufel, T. (1998) *SAP R/3 Process-oriented implementation.* Addison-Wesley Longman, Harlow.

Koch, C., Slater, D. and Baatz, E. (2001) The ABCs of ERP. *CIO Magazine,* 22 December. Reprinted in Fahy, M. (ed), *Enterprise resource planning systems.* CIMA, London, pp. 6–12.

Kotler, P. (2003) *Marketing management,* 11th edition. Prentice-Hall, Englewood Cliffs, NJ.

Lim, B. and Wen, J. (2003) Web services: an analysis of the technology, its benefits, and implementation difficulties. *Inform. Syst. Manag.,* 20(2), 49–57.

Magretta, J. (1998a) The power of virtual integration: an interview with Dell Computer's Michael Dell. *Harv. Bus. Rev.,* 76(2), 73–84.

Magretta, J. (1998b) Fast, global and entrepreneurial: supply chain management, Hong Kong style. *Harv. Bus. Rev.,* 76(5), 102–144.

Martin, I. and Cheung, Y. (2005) Business process re-engineering pays after enterprise resource planning. *Bus. Process Manag. J.,* 11(2), 185–197.

References

Afuah, A. and Tucci, C. (2003) *Business models and strategies.* McGraw-Hill, New York.

Allen, K. (2006) Express Delivery: eBay opens regular online shop. *The Guardian,* 9 October, p. 27.

Anderson, C. (2006) *The long tail: how endless choice is creating unlimited demand.* Random House, London.

Bahli, B. and Ji, F. (2007) An assessment of facilitators and inhibitors for the adoption of enterprise application technology: an empirical study. *Bus. Process. Manag. J.,* 13(1), 108–120.

Baker, W., Marn, M. and Zawada, C. (2001) Price smarter on the net. *Harv. Bus. Rev.,* 79 (2),122–126.

Barriaux, M. (2006) Travellers' fare: scare boosts profits. *The Guardian,* 14 September.

Berners-Lee, T. and Fischetti, M. (1999) *Weaving the web.* Orion Business Books, London.

Berry, M. J. A. and Linoff, G. (1997) *Data mining techniques.* John Wiley and Sons, New York.

Beynon-Davies, P. (2002) *Information systems: an introduction to informatics in organisations.* Palgrave, Basingstoke.

Blackstaff, M. (2006) *Finance for IT decision makers: a practical handbook for buyers, sellers and managers,* 2nd edition. The British Computer Society, Swindon.

Boehm, B. W. (1991) Software risk management: principles and practices. *IEEE Software Mag.,* 8(1), 32–41.

Boersma, K. and Kingma, S. (2005) Developing a cultural perspective on ERP, *Bus. Process Manag. J.,* 11(2), 123–136.

Brignall, M. (2006a) Take this on board, easyJet. *The Guardian Money,* 23 September, p. 10.

Brignall, M. (2006b) uSwitch accused of misleading customers. *The Guardian,* 11 December, p. 21.

Buxman, P., von Ahsen, A., Martin Diaz, L. and Wolf, K. (2004) Usage and evaluation of software supply chain management: results of an empirical stud in the European automotive industry. *Inf. Sys. J.,* 14, 295–309.

Cairncross, F. (2001). *The death of distance 2.0. How the communications revolution will change our lives.* TEXERE Publishing, London.

Chadwick, G. (2005) Bouncing back from oblivion. *Independent on Sunday*, 23 October.

Checkland, P. (1982) *Systems thinking, systems practice.* John Wiley and Sons, Chichester.

Checkland, P. and Holwell, S. (1999) *Information, systems, and information systems.* John Wiley and Sons, Chichester.

Checkland, P. and Scholes, J. (1990) *Soft systems methodology in practice.* John Wiley and Sons, Chichester.

Ciborra, C. U. (1996) The platform organization: recombining strategies, structures and surprises. *Organ. Sci.,* 7(2), 103–117.

Clark, A. (2006) Religious right and sports get their way. *The Guardian,* 3 October, p. 22.

Collinson, P. (2006) Epic of unheroic proportions. *The Money Guardian,* 7 October, p. 4.

Davenport, T. H. (1998) Putting the enterprise into the enterprise system. *Harv. Bus. Rev.,* 76(4), 10–18.

Davis, F. D. (1989) Perceived usefulness, perceived ease of use and user acceptance of information technology. *MIS Quarterly,* 13, 319–339.

Department for Transport (2004) *Making car sharing and car clubs work: a good practice guide.* November 2004. Available at http://www.dft.gov.uk/transportforyou/roads/planning.

Eden, C., Ackerman, F. and Cropper, S. (1992) On the nature of causal maps. *J. Manag. Stud.,* 26(4), 361–378.

Ensor, B. (2006) What stops investors accessing their accounts online? *Forrester Research* 28 August 2006, www.tinyurl.com/kae70 (accessed September 2006).

Evans, P. and Wurster, T. (2000) *Blown to bits: how the new economics of information transform strategy.* Harvard Business Press, Boston, MA.

Everett, C. (2005) Norwich Union aims to make life easier for its staff and customers. *Computing,* 17 November, p. 39.

Fahy, M. (2001) *Enterprise resource planning systems.* CIMA, London.

Fairley, R. (1994) Risk management for software projects. *IEEE Software,* 11(3), 57–67.

Feeny, D. (1997) Information management – lasting ideas within turbulent technology. In Willcocks, L. P., Feeny, D. F. and Islei, G. (eds), *Managing IT as a strategic resource.* McGraw-Hill, Maidenhead.

Fichman, R. and Kemerer, C. F. (1993) Adoption of software process innovations: the case of object orientation. *Sloan Manag. Rev.,* 34, 7–22.

Finch, J. (2006) Viewpoint: never mind the Sarbox, here's the regulator. *The Guardian,* 14 September, p. 29.

Friedlos, D. (2006) AA gets monitoring with identity management. *Computing,* 29 June, p. 4.

Gebauer, J., Shaw, M. J. and Zhao, K. (2002) A different view of IT evaluation – the case of emerging technologies. In Brown, A. and Remenyi, D. (eds), *Proceedings of 9th European Conference on Information Technology Evaluation.* MCIL, Reading, pp. 173–180.

Gilb, T. with Finzi, S. (1988) *Principles of software engineering management.* Addison-Wesley, Wokingham.

Gladwell, M. (2006) *Blink: the power of thinking without thinking.* Penguin, London.

Goodhue, D. L. and Thompson, R. L. (1995) Task-technology fit and industrial performance. *MIS Quarterly,* 19(2), 213–236.

Gow, D. (2006) EC competition chief denies Microsoft vendetta. *The Guardian,* 20 September.

Hagel III, J. (2002) *Out of the box: strategies for achieving profits today an growth tomorrow through web services.* Harvard Business School Pres Boston, MA.

Hagel III, J. and Seely Brown, J. (2001) Your next IT strategy. *Harv. B Rev.,* 79(9), 105–113.

Hamel, G. and Prahalad, C. K. (1989) Strategic Intent. *Harv. Bus. F* 67(3), 63–76.

Hammer, M. and Champy, J. (1993). *Re-engineering the corpora* Nicholas Brealey Publishing, London.

Harris, L. and Dennis, C. (2002) *Marketing the e-business.* Rout e-business, London.

Hilpern, K. (2005) What the experts say. *Independent on Su* 18 December, pp. 16–17.

Hirt, S. G. and Swanson, E. B. (1999) Adopting SAP at Siemans Corporation. *J. Inform. Tech.,* 14, 243–251.

Holt, J. and Newton, J. (eds.) (2004) *A manager's guide to* The British Computer Society, Swindon.

Milmo, D. (2006) Airport security scare costs BAA £13m – and climbing. *The Guardian,* 15 September, p. 24.

Naughton, J. (1999) *A brief history of the future: the origins of the internet.* Weidenfeld and Nicolson, London.

Newell, F. (2000) *loyalty.com.* McGraw-Hill, New York.

Newton, J. (2004) Doing business electronically. In Holt, J. and Newtown, J. (eds.), *A manager's guide to IT law.* The British Computer Society, Swindon.

Odlyzko, A. (2001) Internet pricing and the history of communications. *Comput. Network.,* 36, 493–517.

Office of Government Commerce (2003). *Managing successful programmes.* The Stationery Office, London.

Open Source Initiative (2002) The open source definition version 1.9. www.opensource.org/docs/definition.php.

Payne, A. (ed.) (1995) *Advances in relationship marketing.* Kogan Page, London.

Peters, T. (1988) *Thriving on chaos.* Macmillan. London.

Picton, D. and Broderick, A. (2001) *Integrated marketing communications.* Prentice-Hall, London.

Porter, M. E. (1980) *Competitive strategy.* The Free Press, London.

Porter, M. E. (1985) *Competitive advantage.* The Free Press, London.

Porter, M. E. (2001) Strategy and the internet. *Harv. Bus. Rev.,* 79(3), 62–78.

Prahalad, C. K. and Hamel, G. (1990) The core competence of the corporation. *Harv. Bus. Rev.,* May-June, 79–91.

Quinn, J. B. (1980) Managing strategic change. *Sloan Manag. Rev.,* 21(4), 3–20.

Ray, A. W. and Ray, J. J. (2006) Strategic benefits to SMEs from third party web services: an action research analysis. *J. Strat. Inform. Syst.,* 15, 273–291.

Rogers, E. M. (1983) *Diffusion of innovation.* The Free Press, New York.

Scapens, R., Jazayen, M. and Scapens, J. (1998) SAP: integrated information systems and the implications for management accountants. *Management Accounting: Magazine for Chartered Management Accountants,* 76(8), 46–48.

Scheider, G. P. (2003) *Electronic commerce.* Thompson Course Technology, Boston, MA.

Scheider, P. (1999) Wanted e-people skills. *CIO Magazine,* 1 March. Reprinted in Fahy, M. (ed.) *Enterprise resource planning systems.* CIMA, London, pp. 100–106.

Schulze, C. and Baumgartner, J. (2001) *Don't panic. Do E-commerce.* European Commission, Electronic Commerce Team.

Shehab, E. M., Sharp, M. W., Supramaniam, L. and Spedding, T. A. (2004) Enterprise resource planning: an integrative review. *Bus. Process Manag. J.,* 10(4), 359–386.

Soh, C., Sia Siew Kien and Tay-Yap, J. (2000) Cultural fits and misfits: is ERP a universal solution?' *Commun. ACM,* 43(4), 47–51.

Sprott, D. (2000) Componentizing the enterprise application package. *Commun. ACM,* 43(4), 63–69.

Stabell, C. and Fjeldstad, Ø. (1998) Configuring value for competitive advantage. *Strat. Manag. J.,* 19, 413–437.

Stacey, R. D. (1993) *Strategic management and organizational dynamics.* Pitman Publishing, London.

Stalhane, T., Borgersen, P. C. and Arnesen, K. (1997) In search of the customer's quality view. *J. Syst. Software,* 38(1), 85–97.

Stalk, G., Evans, P. and Schulman, L. E. (1992) Competing on capabilities: the new rules of corporate strategy. *Harv. Bus. Rev.,* 70(2), 57–69.

Stapleton, J. (2002) *DSDM: A framework for business-centred development.* Addison-Wesley, Harlow.

Teece, D. J. (1986) Profiting from technological innovation: implications for integration, collaboration, licensing and public policy. *Research Policy,* 15, 285–305.

Thompson, J. D. (2003) *Organizations in action.* Transaction Publishers, New Brunswick, NJ.

Vogt, C. (2002) Intractable ERP: a comprehensive analysis of failed enterprise-resource-planning projects. *Software Eng. Notes,* 27(2), 62–68.

Watson, J. (2006) Can electricity supplies keep up with growing demand? *Computing* 23 February, 2006, p 15.

Weber, S. (2004) *The success of open source.* Harvard University Press, Cambridge, MA.

Williams, Lara (2006) A change for the better? *Computing* 27th July pp 23–24.

Wray, R. (2006a) Ambush wipes £4b off web shares. *The Guardian,* 3 October, p. 22.

Wray, R. (2006b) HSBC rings in mobile banking. *The Guardian,* 4 October, p. 24.

Yen, B., Fahoomand, A. and Ng, P. (2004) Constructing an e-supply chain at Eastman Chemical Company. *J. Inform. Tech.,* 19, 93–107.

Index